Macr

FLASH MX 2004

for PC/MAC

ISBN : 2-7460-2594-9
Original edition: 2-7460-2470-5

Editions ENI

BP 32125
44021 NANTES Cedex 01 - France

Phone: +33 (0)2 51 80 15 15
Fax: +33 (0)2 51 80 15 16

E-mail: info@eni-publishing.com
http: www.editions-eni.com

English edition: Adrienne TOMMY
Straight to the Point collection directed by Corinne HERVO

Foreword

The aim of this book is to help you find rapidly the features of **Flash MX 2004**, the application for creating vector-based Web animations on PC or Mac. The final pages are given over to an **index** of the topics covered and a **glossary** of terms.

The typographic conventions used in this book are as follows:

Typefaces used for specific purposes:

▷ **bold** indicates the option to take in a menu or dialog box.

▷ *italic* is used for notes and comments.

▷ Ctrl represents a key from the keyboard; when two keys appear side by side, they should be pressed simultaneously.

Symbols indicating the content of a paragraph:

▷ an action to carry out (activating an option, clicking with the mouse...).

⇨ a general comment on the command in question.

a technique which involves the mouse.

A a keyboard technique.

a technique which uses options from the menus.

Table of Contents

OPTIMISATION

PUBLICATION

INDEX

1.1 Overview

A-Starting Flash MX 2004

▷ In Windows go to the **start** menu and activate **All Programs - Macromedia - Macromedia Flash MX 2004**.

▷ On a Mac, use the **Go - Applications** command in the Finder. Open the **Macromedia Flash MX 2004** folder and double-click the **Flash MX 2004** icon.

A welcome page opens.

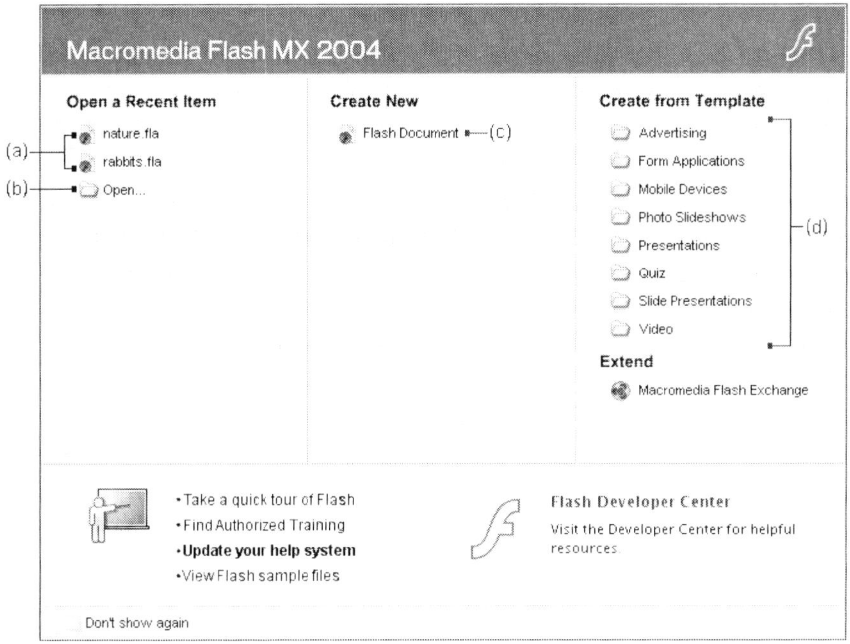

▷ Choose:

(a) to open a document you have worked on recently.

(b) to open an existing document by looking for it in the file hierarchy.

(c) to create a new blank document.

(d) to create a new document using a template selected in one of the available categories.

The document window then appears on the screen.

B - Description of the screen

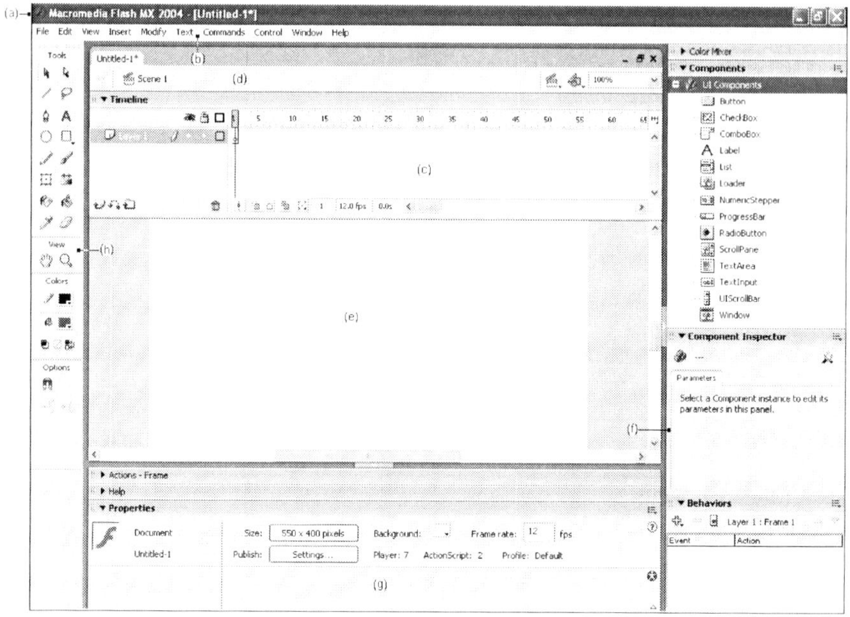

Flash MX 2004 on PC

(a) The title bar.

(b) The menu bar.

(c) The **Timeline** allows you to change the images and layers in an animation.

(d) The **Edit bar**, which tells you the name of the current scene.

(e) The **Stage** is the area where you assemble the different parts of your animation (shapes, text, images etc).

(f) The **Panels** contain settings for various tasks.

(g) The **Property inspector** displays the properties of the document and the various elements that make up the animation.

(h) The **Tools** panel contains different sections: **Tools**, **View**, **Colors**, **Options**.

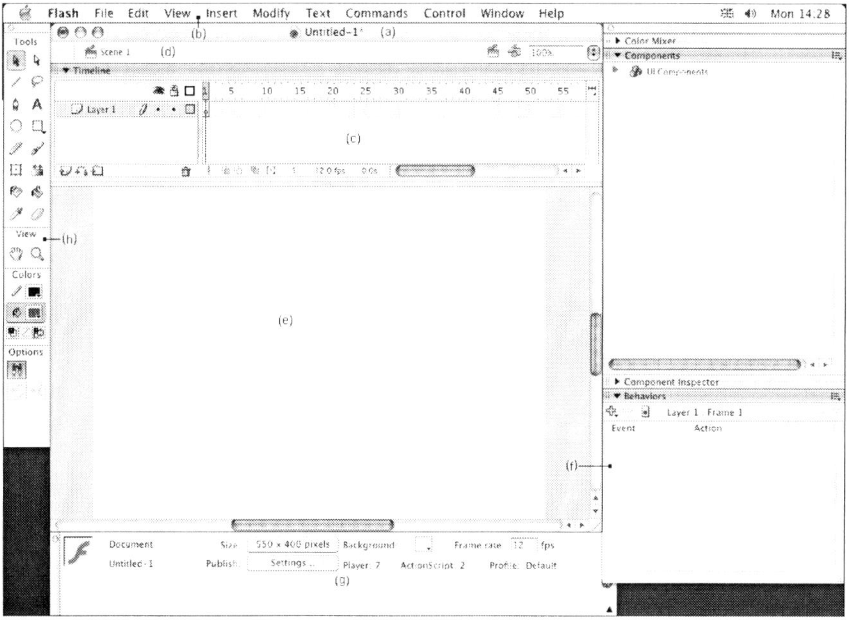

Flash MX 2004 for Mac

⇨ *The **Main** and **Controller** toolbars can be displayed by opening the **Window - Toolbars** menu and ticking the appropriate option:*

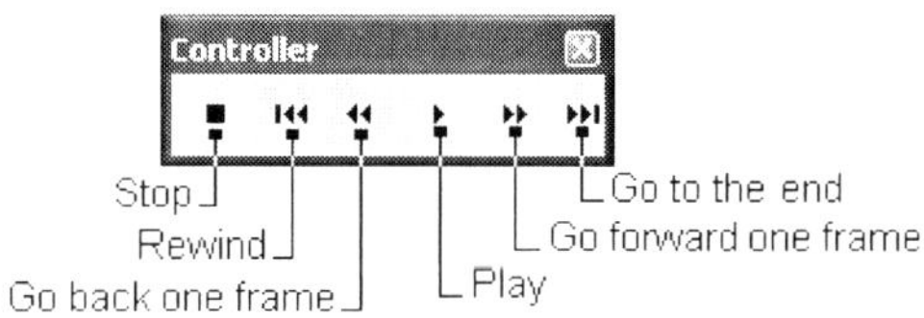

▷ In Mac, you can only show or hide the **Controller** bar using **Window - Toolbars - Controller**.

C - Description of the toolbox

▷ Show or hide the **Tools** panels with:

Window Ctrl F2 (PC)
Tools ⌘ F2 (Mac)

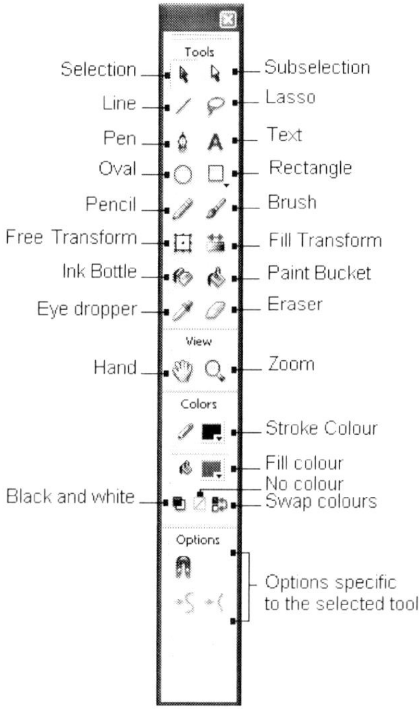

D - Creating, saving and opening a movie

*Documents created in Flash are called **movies**. Under Windows, they carry an **fla** file extension.*

▷ To create a new animation when another is already open:

File Ctrl **N** (PC)
New ⌘ **N** (Mac)

*The **New Document** dialog box opens on the screen.*

▷ To create a blank document, click **Flash Document** on the **General** page.

▷ To create a movie from a template, activate the **Templates** tab.

This changes the name of the dialog box.

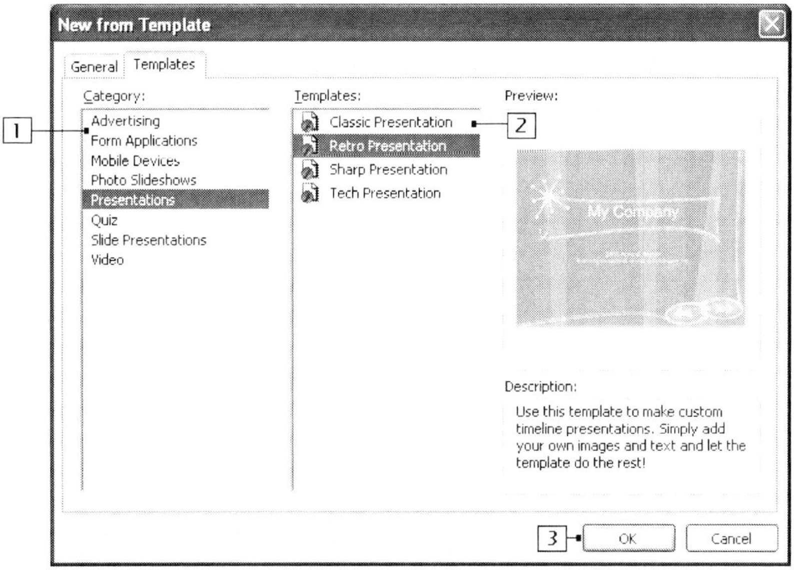

1 Choose the category.

2 Select the required template.

3 Click **OK**.

⇨ *Under Windows, the button directly creates a new movie of the same type as the last movie created.*

▷ To open an existing movie:

File
Open (PC) — Ctrl **O** (PC) / ⌘ **O** (Mac)

On a PC, when several movies are open, each one has a separate window tab. To activate a movie, click its tab:

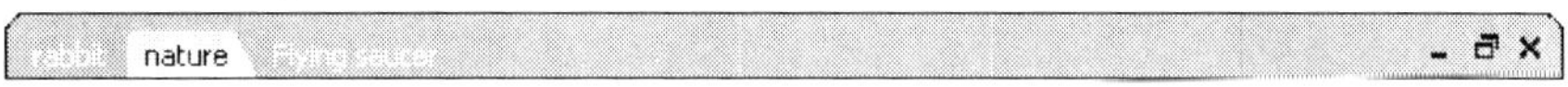

On a Mac, each movie opens in its own window.

▷ To close a movie:

File
Close — (PC) (Mac) on the document window — Ctrl **W** (PC) / ⌘ **W** (Mac)

▷ If necessary, save the last changes you made.

▷ To save a movie:

File
Save (PC) — Ctrl **S** (PC) / ⌘ **S** (Mac)

If this is the first time you have saved it, give a name for the movie and specify in which folder you want to save it.

⇨ *To save a movie under a different name, use **File - Save As** or Ctrl Shift **S** (PC) or ⌘ Shift **S** (Mac).*

⇨ *To create a template based on the current document, use* ***File - Save as Template****. Select a suitable* ***Category****. Give the template a* ***Name*** *and, if you wish, a brief* ***Description*** *then click the* ***Save*** *button.*

E - Setting movie properties

▷ **Modify**
Document

Ctrl **J** (PC)
⌘ **J** (Mac)

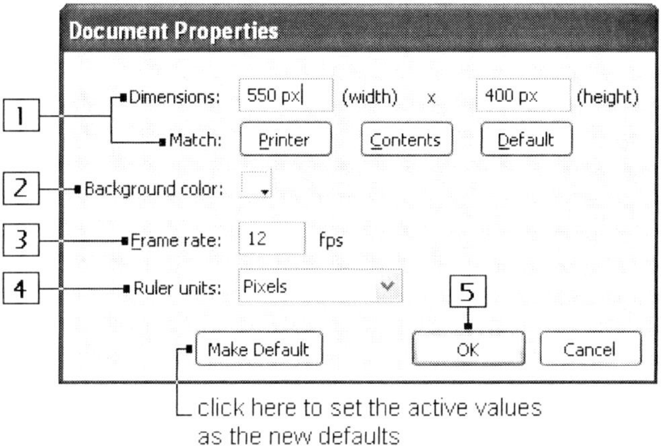

1 Give the movie's **Dimensions**, namely the width and height, or click the **Printer** button if you want the size to match the printing format defined in the page setup options. Click the **Contents** button to adjust the movie's size to the items in every scene.

2 Choose the background colour for the movie, using the colour picker.

3 Specify how many frames per second you require.

4 Select the ruler's measurement unit.

5 Click to confirm.

⇨ *The options also appear in the Property inspector, providing there is no active selection.*

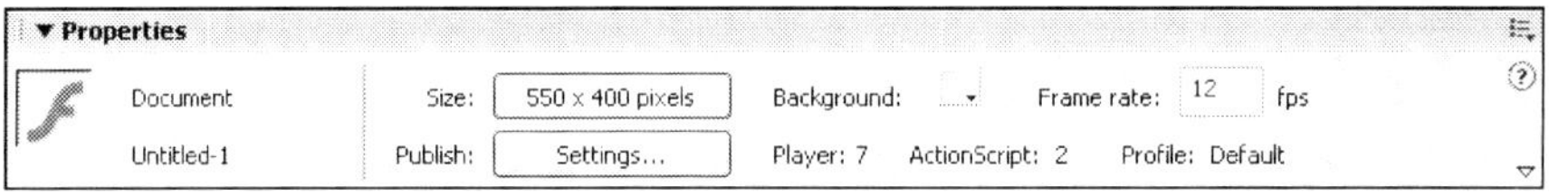

F - Cancelling/redoing actions

▷ Display the **History** panel:

Window
Other Panels
History

Ctrl F10 (PC)
⌘ F10 (Mac)

▷ To cancel the last actions you performed, drag the slider upwards, to grey out the actions you wish to cancel.

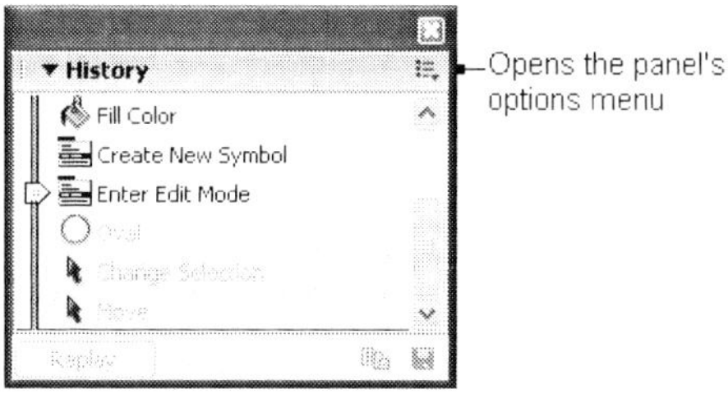

The effects can immediately be seen on the stage.

▷ To repeat one or several actions, select the elements concerned on the stage.
In the **History** panel, select the actions you wish to carry out again: click the first action, hold down the [⇧ Shift] key and click the last action, before releasing the key.
Click the **Replay** button on the panel.

⇒ *The* [undo] *and* [redo] *buttons on the **Main** toolbar can also be used to cancel or repeat the last actions you carried out, but you need to keep clicking the button for several actions.*

⇒ *The default number of possible "undos" is 100, but you can change these in the Flash preferences (cf. 1.5 - A - Defining the preferences).*

⇒ *To erase the contents of the history for the active document, open the **History** panel's options menu and click **Clear History**.*

1.2 Panels

A - Managing panels

▷ To display a panel, click the **Window** menu and then:

Design Panels	to display the list of panels used for graphics work.
Development Panels	to display the list of panels linked to programming work.
Other Panels	to display a list of miscellaneous panels.

▷ Click the name of the required panel.

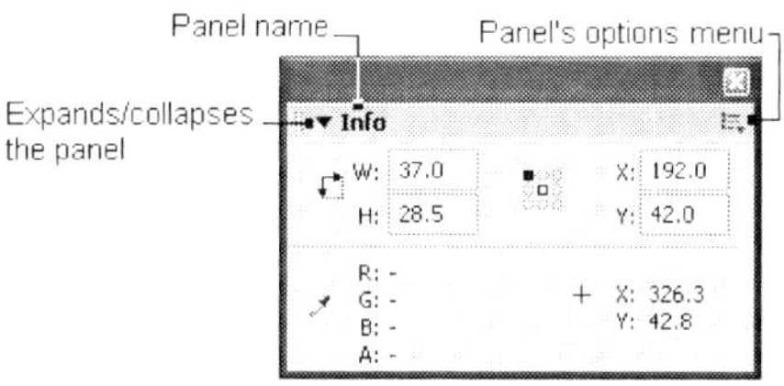

***Info** panel on a PC*

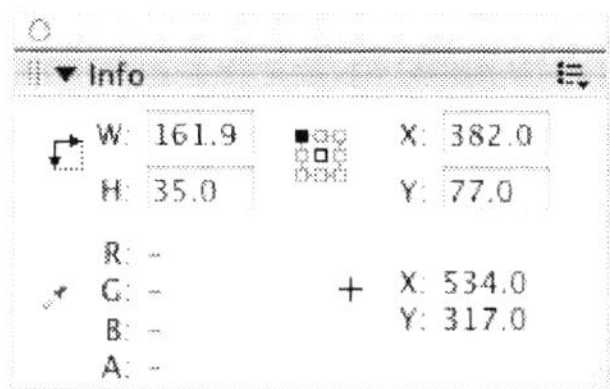

***Info** panel on a Mac*

▷ To move a fixed panel, drag it by its [grip] button.
It becomes a floating panel: a title bar appears on it.

To fix a panel again, simply drag it one of the edges of the application window.

▷ To resize a floating panel, drag one of its corners.

▷ To expand or collapse a panel, click the small triangle to the left of the panel's name:

You can also expand or collapse a panel by clicking its name.

▷ To close a panel, activate the **Close Panel** option in the panel's options menu or click its close button. To close all the panels, use the appropriate option in the **Window** menu.

⇨ *You can hide or display all open panels by pressing the* F4 *key.*

B - The Property inspector

*The **Property inspector** shows the settings for the current object, or if nothing is selected, those for the document.*

▷ To display/hide the Property inspector, use **Window - Properties** or Ctrl F3 (PC) or ⌘ F3 (Mac).

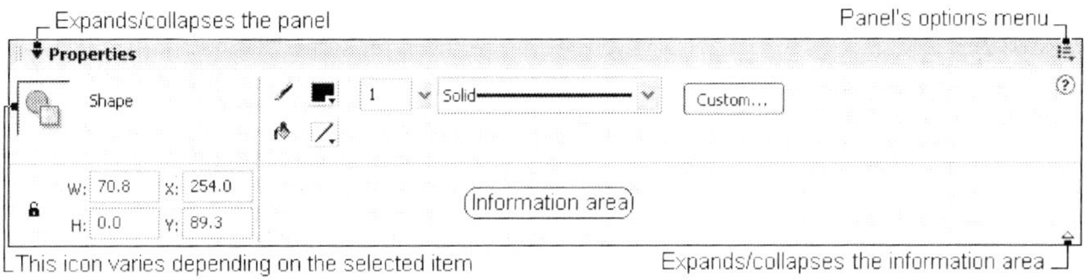

C - The Timeline

The Timeline contains layers and frames. Layers are a way of managing independently different objects that are on the stage. At any given time, you will see the items from the various visible layers on the stage. When you play a movie, the playhead moves from frame to frame and the stage's contents change according to what items have been placed on the layers in each frame of the Timeline.

▷ To display/hide the **Timeline** panel:

Window
Timeline

Ctrl Alt **T** (PC)
⌘ ⌥ **T** (Mac)

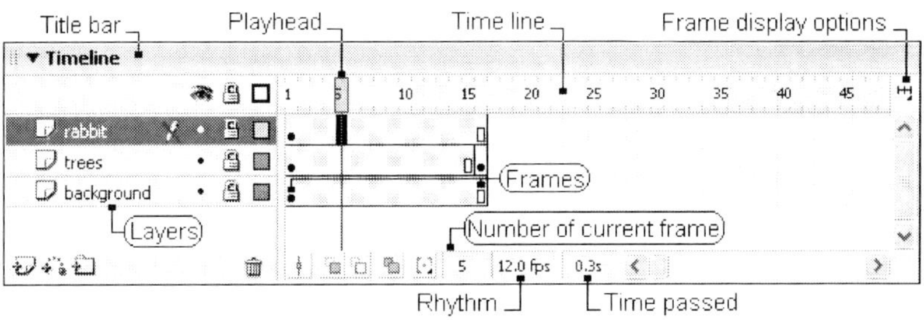

D-Using panel sets

If you like to customise your workspace, by laying out the panels and windows or changing the screen resolution for your own needs, it would be useful for you to save the workspace layout by creating a panel set.

▷ Set out the panels and windows as you want then to be, then use the **Window - Save Panel Layout** command.

▷ Give your new panel set a **Name**.

▷ To use a saved panel set, use **Window - Panel Sets**.

▷ Click the name of the set you wish to use.

*The **Default Layout** option retrieves the original layout of the panels.*

⇨ *To delete a panel set, delete the file for it in the Panel Sets folder that is within the program folders for the Flash MX 2004 application.*

1.3 Views and snapping modes

A-Activating a view

The selected view determines the screen rendering qualities and the speed with which the document displays.

▷ Take one of these options from the **View - Preview Mode** menu:

Outlines	Only the outlines of objects are visible.
Fast	Applies no anti-aliasing: shows only line styles and colours.
Antialias	Smoothes the edges of graphics, shapes and bitmap drawings.
Antialias Text	Smoothes the edges of text. This is the default mode, but it tends to slow display if your document contains a lot of text.
Full	Provides complete rendering of the objects on the stage. This tends to slow display.

B-Changing the zoom level

▷ Select the **Zoom** tool, click the **Enlarge** or **Reduce** option and click the item you wish to zoom. You can also drag over the area you wish to zoom.

⇨ *The* Alt *(PC) or* ⌥ *(Mac) key can be pressed to toggle between **Enlarge** and **Reduce** modes.*

▷ You can also use the **View - Magnification** menu:

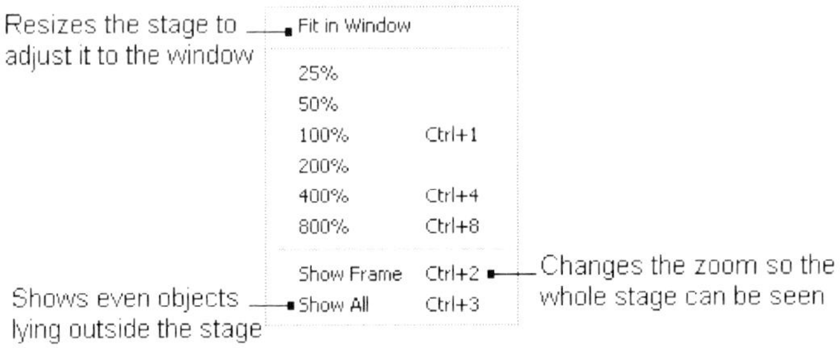

⇨ *You can also select a zoom level from the drop-down list on the **Edit bar** above the stage.*

⇨ *The **M** and **Z** keys activate the **Zoom** tool.*

⇨ *If you cannot see a certain part of the stage, select the **Hand** tool and drag the stage (you can activate the **Hand** tool by pressing **H** on the keyboard, or, to turn it on temporarily, by holding down the space bar).*

C - Showing/hiding the rulers

▷ **View**
Rulers

Ctrl Alt Shift **R** (PC)
⌘ ⌥ Shift **R** (Mac)

The unit on the rulers (pixels by default) is the one you chose in the movie properties.

D - Managing guides

A guide (a horizontal or vertical line) enables you to place objects precisely on the stage.

▷ Display the rulers if necessary.

▷ To create a horizontal or vertical guide, activate the tool, point to the horizontal or vertical ruler and drag the guide onto the stage.

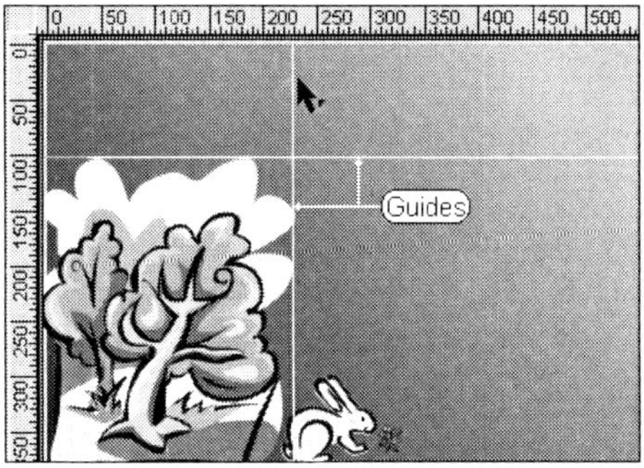

▷ To move a guide, select the tool, point to the guide and drag it to the required position.

⇒ *If a guide is locked, you cannot move it.*

▷ To activate/deactivate guides, use:

View
Guides
Show Guides

Ctrl ; (PC)
⌘ ; (Mac)

▷ To delete a guide, select the tool, point to the guide and drag it onto the ruler.

▷ To lock/unlock the guides:

View
Guides
Lock Guides

Ctrl Alt ; (PC)
⌘ ⌥ ; (Mac)

▷ To activate/deactivate snapping to the guides:

View
Snapping
Snap to Guides

Ctrl ⇧Shift ; (PC)
⌘ ⇧Shift ; (Mac)

When this is active, objects that you move are pulled towards the guides.

⇒ *To change the preferences for the guides, use **View - Guides - Edit Guides** or Ctrl Alt ⇧Shift **G** (PC) or ⌘ ⌥ ⇧Shift **G** (Mac).*

E - Using the grid

Like the guides, the grid is there to help you position objects correctly on the stage.

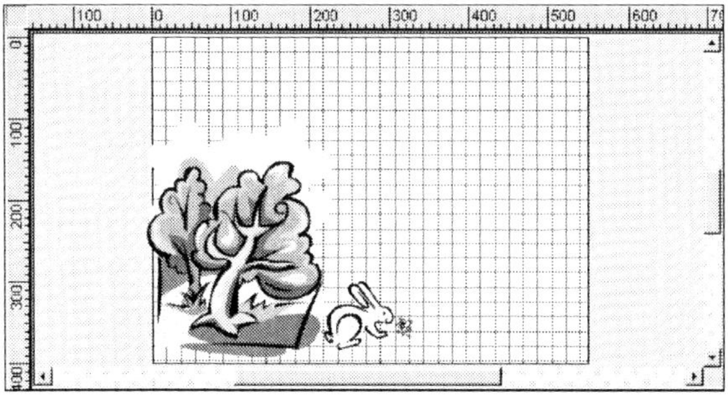

▷ To display/hide the grid:

View [Ctrl] **#** (PC)
Grid [⌘] **'** (Mac)
Show Grid

▷ To activate/deactivate snapping to the grid:

View [Ctrl][⇧ Shift] **#** (PC)
Snapping [⌘][⇧ Shift] **'** (Mac)
Snap to Grid

When this is active, objects that you move are pulled towards the gridlines.

⇨ *To change the preferences for the grid, use **View - Grid - Edit Grid** or [Ctrl][Alt] **G** (PC) or [⌘][⌥] **G** (Mac).*

⇨ *The **Snap to Pixels** option in the **View - Snapping** menu displays a pixel grid so you can snap objects down to a pixel. To see this grid, you need to use a high zoom level (at least 400%). On a PC, the **X** key temporarily hides the pixel grid when it is on display and the **C** key toggles this snapping mode temporarily.*

F - Snapping objects

The objective of snapping is to help you position objects in relation to each other.

▷ **View** [Ctrl][⇧ Shift] / (PC)
Snapping [⌘][⇧ Shift] / (Mac)
Snap to Objects

The snapping point is defined by the point where you click the object. It is symbolized by a small black circle that grows bigger as you move the object near a "snapable" zone.

⇨ ***Snap to Objects** mode is the most frequently-used mode; you can activate or deactivate it quickly using the*  *option in the **Options** section of the **Tools** panel when some tools are active such as* .

G - Using snap alignment

In this mode, guides appear on the screen as you move objects to show you the edges of bounding boxes or object centres to facilitate snapping. You can define the snapping tolerance, which states how close objects have to be before they will snap.

▷ To set the snap alignment preferences:

View
Snapping
Edit Snap Align

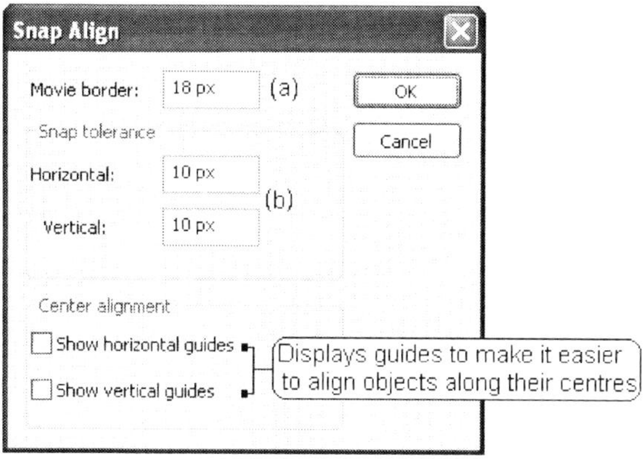

▷ Set the snapping tolerance:

(a) Between the object being moved and the edge of the stage.

(b) Between the horizontal or vertical edges of the objects.

▷ Click **OK**.

▷ To activate the snap alignment feature:

View
Snapping
Snap Align

1.4 Layers

A-Managing layers

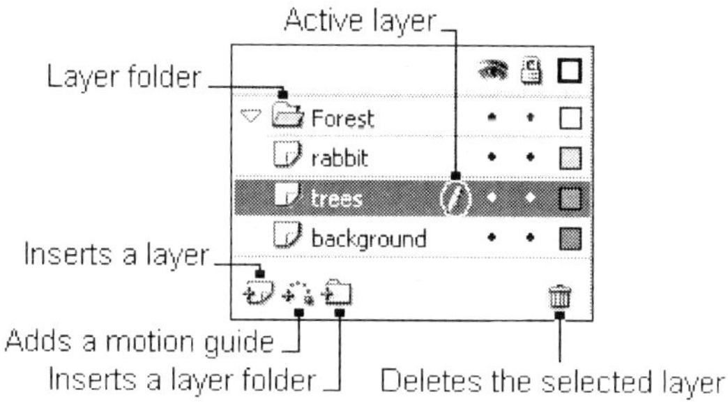

▷ To create a layer, select the layer above which you want to position the new layer then use the **Insert - Timeline - Layer** command or click the button at the bottom of the **Timeline**.

You can also use the shortcut menu.

▷ To manage layers, use the buttons to the right of the layer's name:

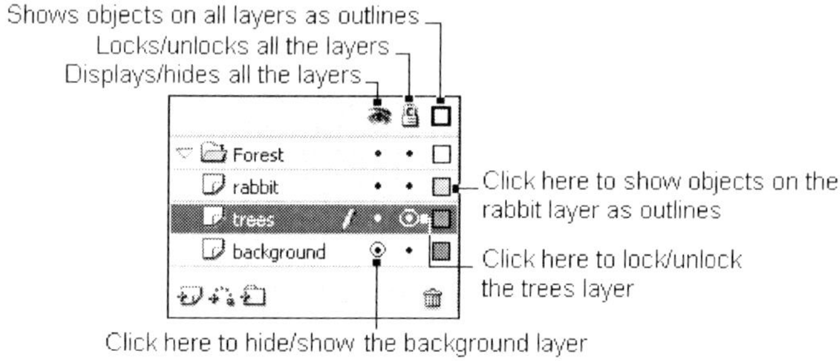

When you display layers as outlines, only object outlines appear, in the colour that is connected with the layer.

When you hide a layer, a [X] *icon appears in its column.*

▷ To move a layer, drag it upwards or downwards.

▷ To select a layer, click it: the [pencil] icon means that a layer is active.

To select several layers, use the [Shift] key as you click, if they are adjacent, or the [Ctrl] (PC) or [⌘] (Mac) key if they are far apart.

▷ To rename a layer, double-click its name, type the new name and press [Enter].

▷ To delete a layer, select it by clicking its name, then click the [trash] icon, or simply drag the layer onto this trash icon.

⇨ *If you hold down the* [Alt] *(PC) or* [⌥] *(Mac) key as you click one of the columns, you activate or deactivate that property for all layers except the active layer. You can also use the* ***Hide Others*** *or* ***Lock Others*** *command from a layer's shortcut menu.*

B - Changing a layer's properties

▷ Select the layer.

▷ **Modify - Timeline - Layer Properties**

You can also double-click the icon to the left of the layer's name in the Timeline.

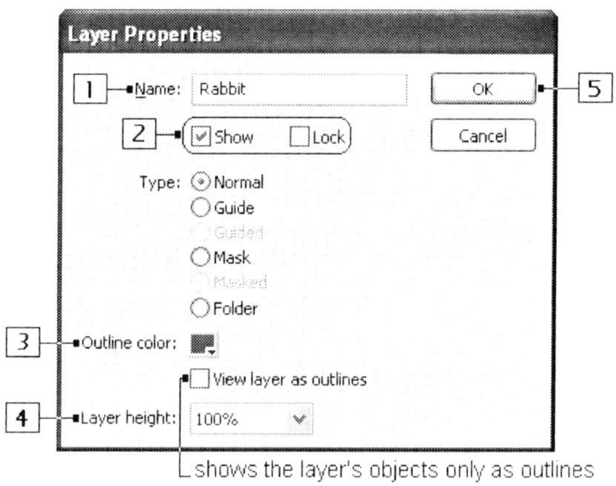

1 Give the layer's name.

2 Choose whether to display and/or lock the layer.

3 Select the colour that will be used when layers are viewed as outlines.

4 Define the height of the layer.

5 Click to confirm the properties.

C - Creating layer folders

You can group several layers into a layer folder to organise your layers more efficiently.

▷ Select the layer above which the new layer folder should appear.

▷ **Insert - Timeline - Layer Folder** or click the icon.

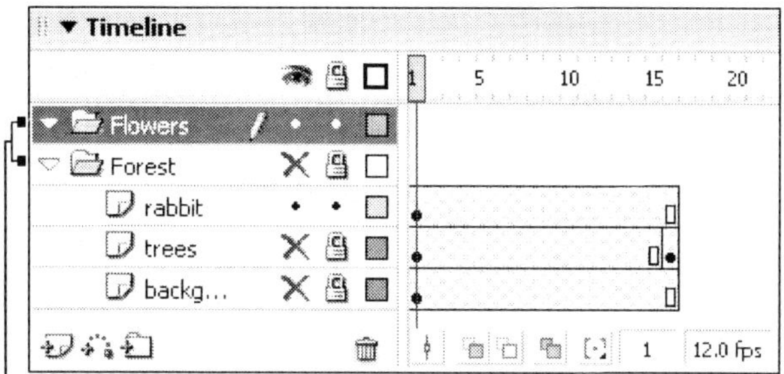

Click here to open or close a folder

▷ To place a layer within the folder, simply drag it in.

▷ To expand or collapse all the layer folders, activate the **Expand All Folders** or **Collapse All Folders** option from the shortcut menu.

⇨ *Layer folders can be managed like layers.*

1.5 Setting Flash MX 2004 general options

A - Defining the preferences

▷ **Edit** (PC)/**Flash** (Mac)
Preferences

Ctrl **U** (PC)
⌘ **U** (Mac)

General tab

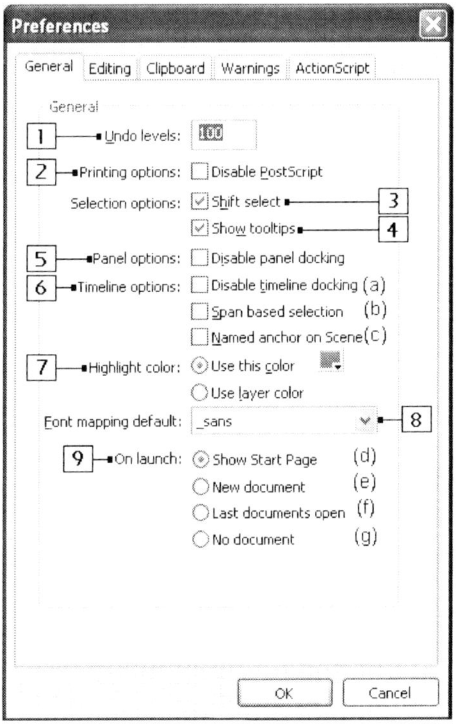

1 Enter how many actions can be undone (between 0 and 9999).

2 Activate this option if your PostScript printer is having printing problems (PC only).

3 If you deactivate this option, you can select several objects without having to use the Shift key.

4 Do you want screen tips to display when you point to items?

5 Activate this option if you do not want panels to embed themselves with other panels as you move them (PC only).

6 Set the timeline options:

(a) Do you want to stop the timeline being anchored to the edges of the window?

(b) When you select a single frame, the entire span will be selected.

(c) The first frame in each sequence will have a named anchor.

7 Choose the highlighting colour for selected objects.

8 Select the font used to replace movie fonts that are not installed on your system.

9 Specify what Flash should do when it first starts: display the start page (d) or one of the following:

(e) Automatically create a new blank document.

(f) Load the last documents open in the application.

(g) Display nothing.

Editing tab

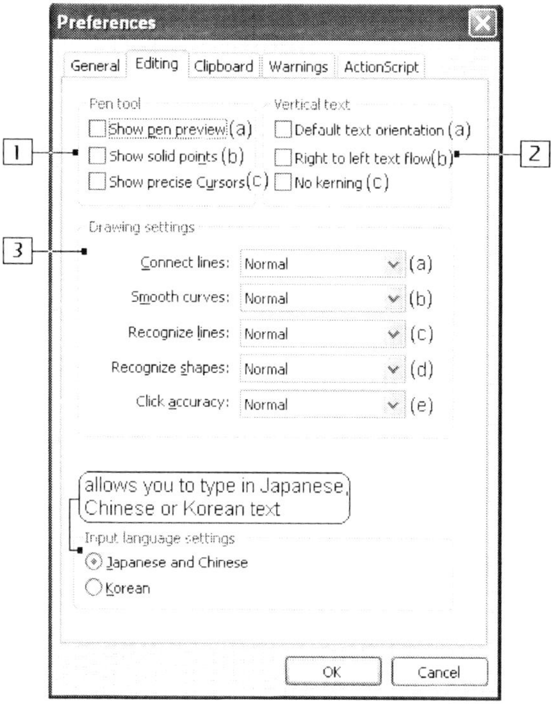

1 Define the settings for the **Pen Tool**:

(a) to see a preview of the line you will draw before you start to draw it.

(b) to switch the appearance of selected points. Normally, selected points are empty and solid points represent unselected ones.

(c) to use a cross rather than the **Pen** icon.

2 Set the options for vertical text:

(a) should vertical text be the default orientation? This can be useful for some Asian fonts.

(b) sshould text be entered from right to left? This is useful for certain Middle-Eastern languages.

(c) this turns character kerning on or off.

3 Use the following options to define the drawing settings:

(a) Sets how far apart two extremities need to be before they connect.

(b) The smoothing level applied to curves drawn with the Pencil tool.

(c) Adjusts the position of the points so that the path drawn is as straight as possible.

(d) If some lines look like geometric shapes, Flash will adjust them, making them rectangles, ovals, etc.

(e) Defines how far away the pointer needs to be from an object for it to be recognised and selected.

Clipboard tab

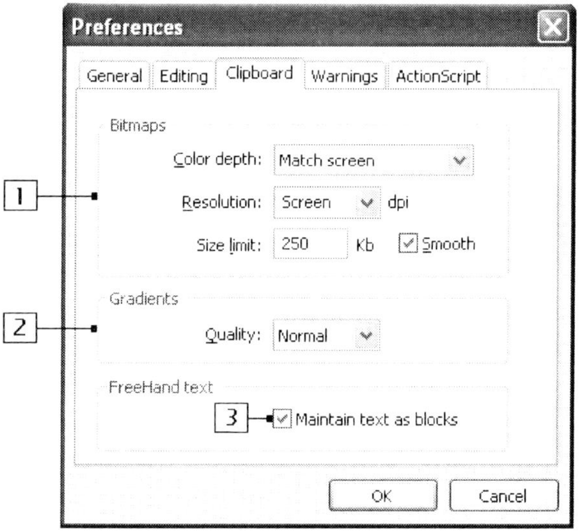

Clipboard tab - PC

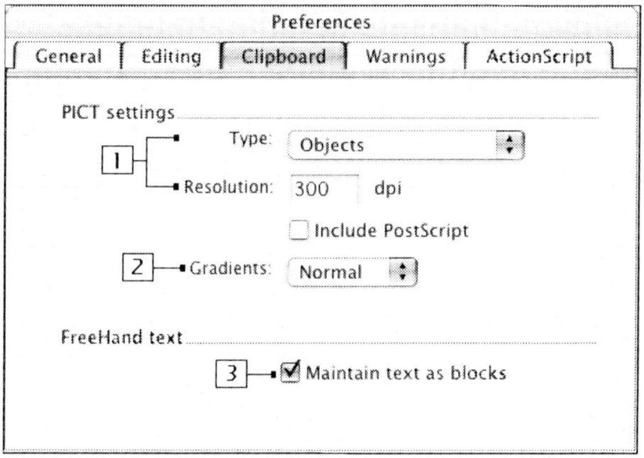

Clipboard tab - Mac

1 Define the settings for bitmap images that you copy into Flash MX 2004.

2 Set the quality for gradient fills.

3 Activate this option to preserve text as a block when you copy it in Freehand.

Warnings tab

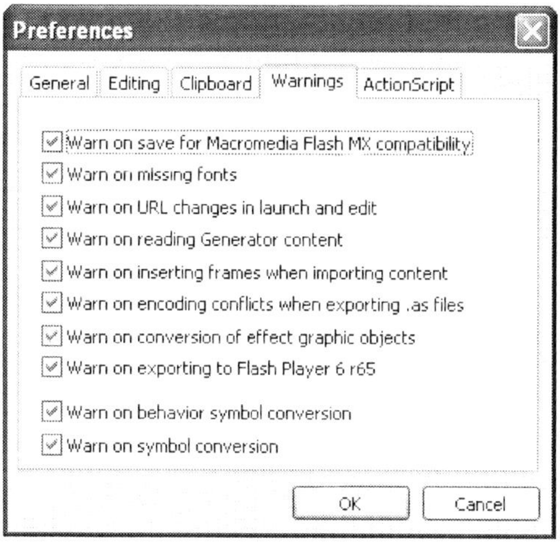

All the warning options are active by default.

▷ Deactivate the warning options that do not interest you.

⇨ *The **ActionScript** tab contains view options for editing ActionScript.*

B - Customising the shortcut keys

▷ **Edit** (PC)/**Flash** (Mac)

Keyboard Shortcuts

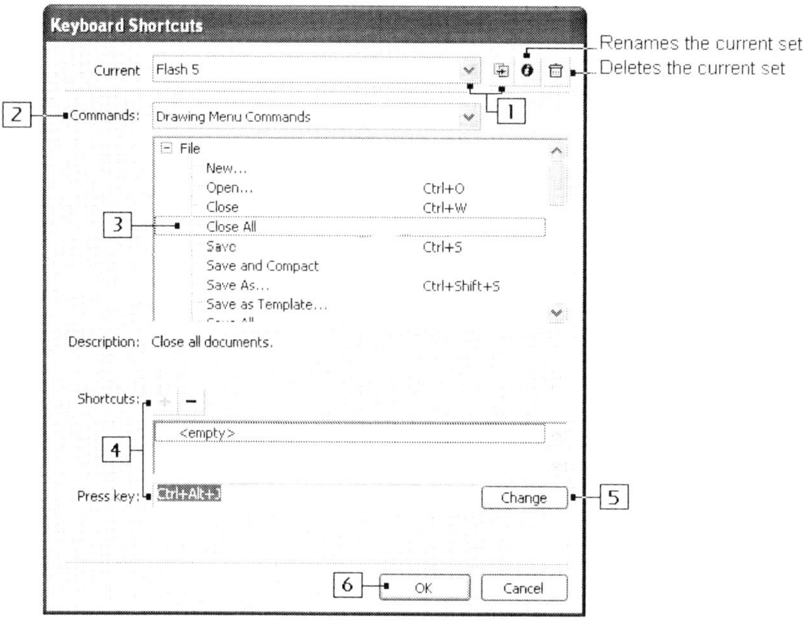

1 Select an existing set of shortcuts or duplicate a set.

2 Choose the category of commands to which you want to add the shortcut.

3 Expand the hierarchy of commands and choose the one concerned.

4 Click the + button and press the shortcut key on the keyboard to enter it in the **Press key** text box.

5 Click this button to change the shortcut.

6 Click **OK** to confirm.

2.1 Drawing

A-Drawing with the Pencil tool

▷ Select the **Pencil** tool.

▷ Define the stroke settings using the Property inspector.

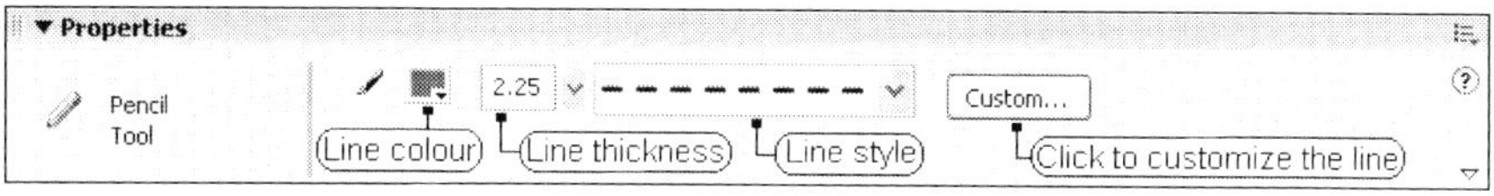

▷ In the **Options** section of the **Tools** panel, select the required mode:

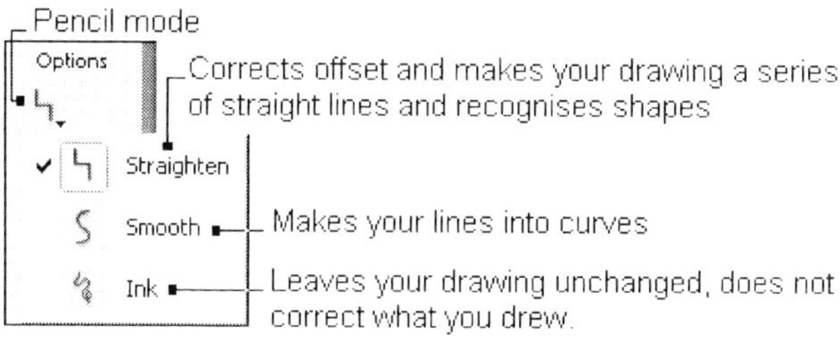

▷ Draw your line by dragging. To draw perfectly straight vertical or horizontal lines, hold down the Shift key as you draw.

B-Using the Line tool

▷ Click the tool button or press the **N** key on the keyboard.

▷ Choose the colour, thickness and style for the line using the Property inspector.

▷ Point to the line starting point on the stage and drag the pointer to draw the line. Hold down the Shift key as you drag to draw a perfectly horizontal, vertical or diagonal line.

C-Drawing an oval or a circle

▷ Click the tool button or press the **O** key on the keyboard.

▷ Choose the **Stroke Color** and **Fill Color** from the **Tools** panel or the Property inspector. Choose the line thickness and style in the Property inspector.

▷ Drag to draw the oval. To draw a circle, hold down the Shift key as you drag.

⇨ *One of the peculiarities of Flash is that when you draw a shape on top of another shape, and both are on the same layer, the topmost area at the intersection of the two shapes is erased. Once you have created a shape, the stroke and fill are independent of each other.*

⇨ *Fill can be a colour, a gradient or a bitmap (cf. 2.2 - Filling a shape with a bitmap image or 2.3 - Applying a gradient to one or more shapes).*

D - Drawing a rectangle or a square

▷ Click the tool button or press the **R** key on the keyboard.

▷ If you wish to make a rectangle/square with rounded corners, click the button in the **Options** sections of the **Tools** panel.

▷ Choose the **Stroke Color** and **Fill Color** from the **Tools** panel or the Property inspector. Choose the line thickness and style in the Property inspector.

▷ Drag to draw the rectangle. To draw a square, hold down the Shift key as you drag.

E - Drawing a polygon or a star

▷ Click and hold down the mouse button over the tool button until the hidden tool appears. Release the mouse and click the tool (or drag straight on that tool on a Mac).

▷ Click the **Options** button on the Property inspector.

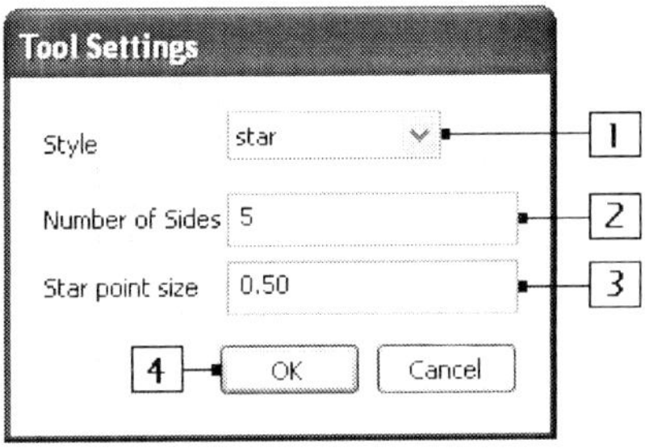

1 Open the list and choose to draw a **star** or **polygon**.

2 Give the number of sides, for a polygon, or the number of points, for a star.

3 If creating a star, enter a value between 0 and 1 to determine the size of the points: 0 applies the maximum size and 0.5 is the default.

4 Click to confirm.

▷ Choose the **Stroke Color** and **Fill Color** from the **Tools** panel or the Property inspector. Choose the line thickness and style in the Property inspector.

▷ Drag on the stage to draw the shape.

⇨ *When you create a shape with the , or tool, you can deactivate the fill colour and/or stroke line. In the **Colors** area of the **Tools** panel, click the **Fill Color** or **Stroke Color** icon (click to the left of the colour swatch) and then the **No Color** icon.*

F - Drawing with the Pen tool

*The **Pen** tool is used to draw very precise lines, made up of straight segments and curves.*

Creating straight segments

▷ Select the tool.

▷ Select the line characteristics using the Property inspector.

▷ Click the stage to create the first point of the segment.

▷ Click where you want to position the segment's second point. Click again to create further segments.

▷ If you want to make a closed path, click back on the first point (the pointer will display a small circle): the path becomes a shape and it will use the active fill colour. If you want to keep the path open, press the [Esc] key.

*The **Pen** tool will stay active.*

Creating curves

▷ Select the tool.

▷ Select the line characteristics using the Property inspector.

▷ Click the stage to place the first point and drag to define the direction of the curved segment.

An anchor point and tangents appear.

▷ Click where you want to place the second point and drag to define the curve. You can invert the curve's direction depending on which way you drag.

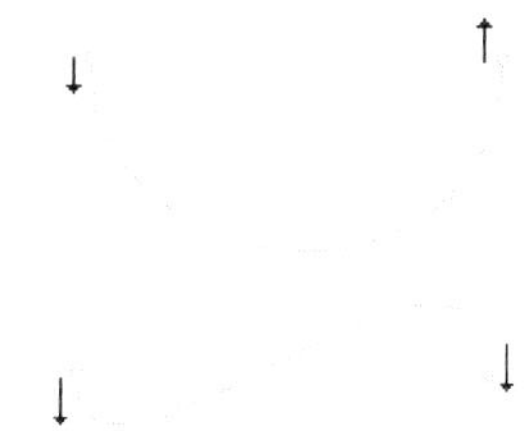

The arrows indicate the dragging direction as each point was drawn. The curve's tangents appear as you drag.

▷ Create each point on the curve in the same way.

▷ To finish the path, either click the first point again, or if you want to keep an open path, press the Esc key.

*The **Pen** tool will stay active.*

⇨ *If you close the shape, it will automatically be filled with the active fill.*

G-Using the Brush tool

Drawing

*The **Brush** tool is used to make lines resembling those of a paintbrush or marker pen and can create calligraphic effects.*

▷ Select the  tool.

▷ On the **Tools** panel, select a **Fill Color** by clicking the associated colour swatch.

▷ Open the **Brush Size** list in the options, to select the required size for your brush.

▷ Open the **Brush Shape** list in the options, to select the shape you want for your brush.

▷ Drag across the stage to draw the line. To draw a horizontal or vertical line, hold down the ⇧ Shift key as you drag.

⇨ *If you use a pressure-sensitive tablet connected to your computer, you can vary the stroke width and angle using the pressure and tilt modifiers.*

Painting items on the stage

▷ Select the  tool.

▷ On the **Tools** panel, select a **Fill Color** by clicking the associated colour swatch.

▷ Click the  icon in the **Options** area and select a painting mode:

 Paints over existing elements, deleting them.

 Paints empty areas and fills, but does not affect lines.

 Paints empty areas behind existing areas.

 Paints selected areas of elements.

 Paints inside the area where you click with the Brush.

▷ Drag the pointer on the stage to paint.

2.2 Modifying lines and shapes

A shape is made up of at least a stroke and/or a fill and it can be selected independently. A line is characterized by a style, thickness and colour. A fill can be a solid colour, a gradient or a bitmap image.

A-Changing a shape's anchor points

▷ Select the **Subselection** tool and click the edge of the shape or line that you want to modify.

The anchor points appear.

▷ To move an anchor point and modify the shape, drag the point (you can also click the point and press the arrow keys).

▷ To move the shape, point to its edge (the ■ sign appears next to the pointer) then drag, or click and use the arrow keys.

▷ To modify a curve, click an anchor point and drag one of the tangent points (the blue circles). To modify one of the tangent points without changing the other, hold down Alt (PC) or ⌥ (Mac) as you drag.

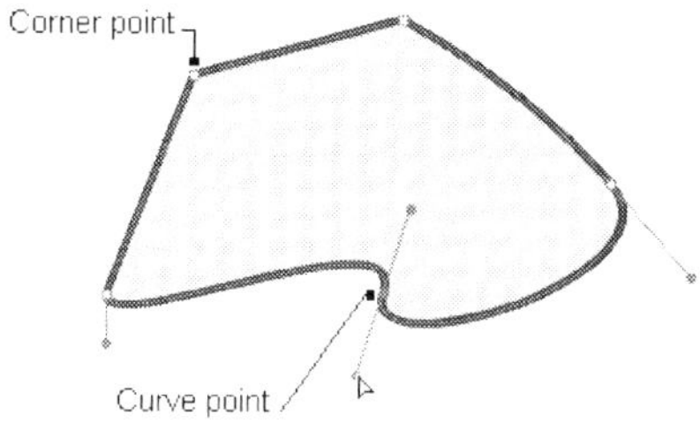

▷ To delete an anchor point, select it with the **Subselection** tool and press the Del key.

You can use ⇧Shift -clicks to select several anchor points.

▷ To add an anchor points, select the **Pen** tool and click the curve or the shape outline to select (a + sign appears near the pointer). Click the place where you want to add the point.

▷ To transform a curve point (with tangents) into a corner point, select the **Pen** tool and click the point (if it is a curve point, a symbol appears with the pointer; if it is a corner point, a — symbol appears).

⇨ *The tool can also be used to change a shape by dragging its outline. If the dragged point is a curve, the pointer is like this ; if it is a corner, the pointer is like this .*

B - Changing a shape's envelope

▷ Select the shape concerned.

▷ **Modify - Transform - Envelope** or click the **Free Transform** tool and click the **Envelope** button in the **Options** area.

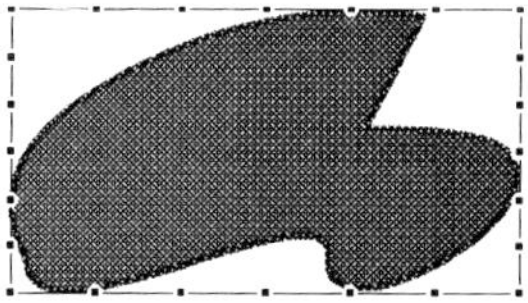

▷ Drag the anchor points and/or tangent points to make the transformation.

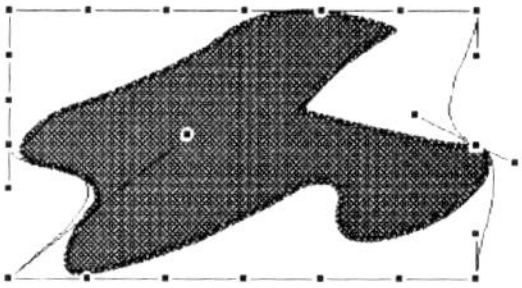

⇨ *You cannot use the **Envelope** modifier to modify symbols, bitmaps or grouped objects.*

C - Smoothing/straightening a shape

▷ Select the shape with the tool.

▷ Click the **Smooth** or **Straighten** button in the **Options** area.

D - Optimising a shape

Optimising a shape reduces the size of the host movie file. The smoothing process reduces the number of curves used.

▷ Select the shape.

▷ **Modify**
Shape
Optimize

Ctrl Alt ⇧Shift **C** (PC)
⌘ ⌥ ⇧Shift **C** (Mac)

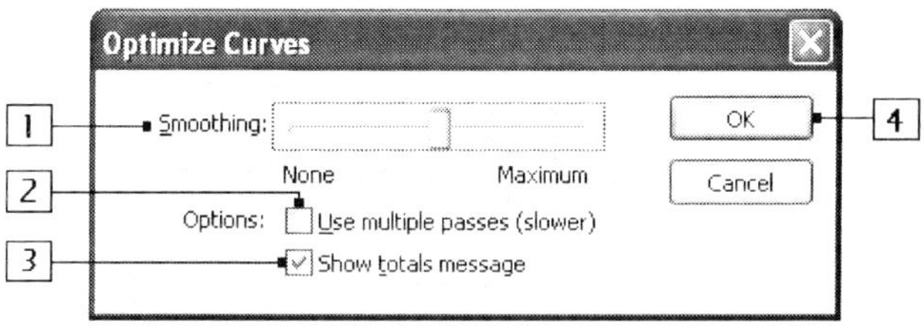

1 Set the degree of smoothing.

2 Tick this option if you want optimization to occur with a maximum degree of smoothing.

3 Tick this option to display a message giving the number of curves before and after smoothing.

4 Click to confirm.

E- Modifying the stroke of a line or a shape

▷ Select the **Ink Bottle** tool.

▷ Choose a **Stroke color**, a thickness and/or a **Stroke style** in the Property inspector.

▷ If you want to modify the selected line style, click the **Custom** button. The settings that appear in the **Stroke Style** dialog box depend on the chosen style.

▷ Change the settings as required and click **OK**.

▷ Click the shape in question.

⇨ *To remove a shape's stroke, select the stroke by double-clicking it with the tool and then press the* Del *key.*

F- Changing a shape's fill

▷ Select the **Paint Bucket** tool.

▷ Choose a **Fill Color** in the **Tools** panel or in the Property inspector.

▷ In the **Options** area of the **Tools** panel, click the icon:

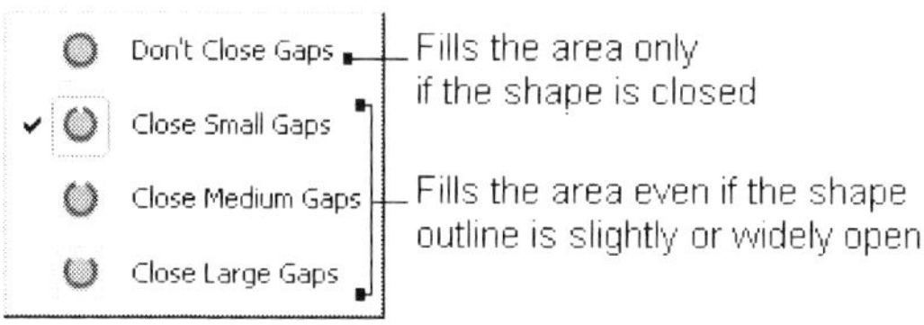

The size of the gap is relative to the zoom being used.

▷ Click the shape.

⇨ *You can also apply a gradient to a shape (cf. 2.3. Colours and gradients).*

G-Filling a shape with a bitmap image

Inserting the bitmap image

▷ **Window** ⇧Shift F9
Design Panels
Color Mixer

▷ Choose **Bitmap** in the drop-down **Fill style** list.

*If there is no bitmap image in the Library, the **Import to Library** dialog box opens.*

▷ Go to the folder containing the bitmap image then double-click the image's name.

*The bitmap appears in the **Color Mixer** panel. It is also inserted into the Library:*

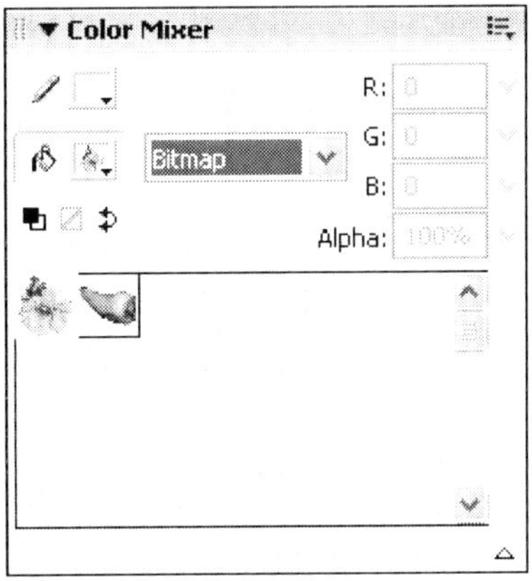

▷ Click the bitmap you wish to use for the fill.

*The image appears in the **Fill color***  *square on the panel.*

▷ Select the **Paint Bucket** tool , set its **Options** and click the shape you wish to fill.

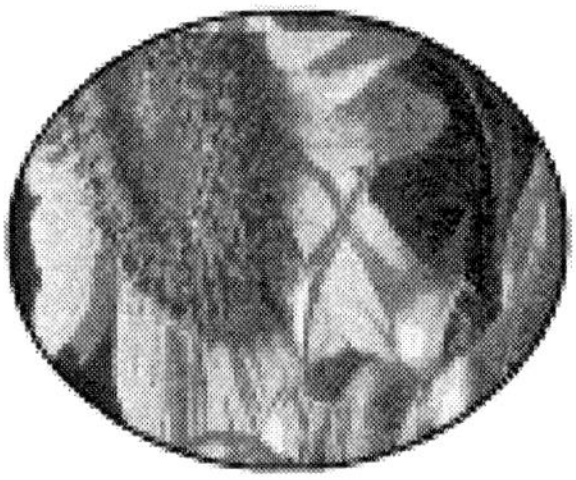

It may occur that the bitmap needs to be repeated several times to fill the shape (that is not the case here). To avoid this tiled effect, you need to change the bitmap's size by changing the fill settings.

Defining the bitmap settings

▷ Select the **Fill Transform** tool  and click the shape.

▷ Drag the various handles:

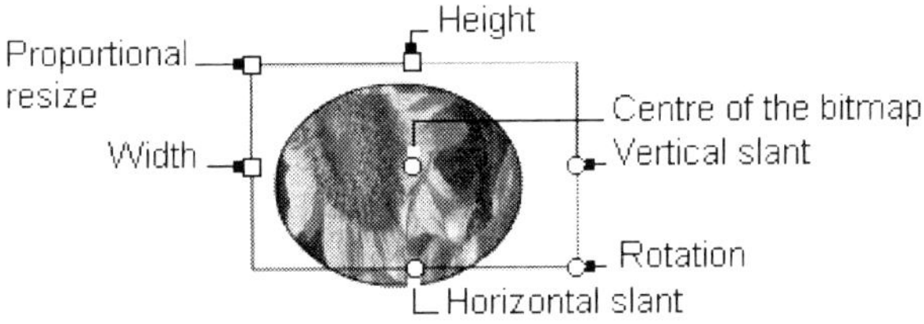

H-Applying the fill or stroke from one shape to another

▷ Select the **Eyedropper** tool  and click the fill or stroke that you want to apply.

*The pointer turns into a **Paint Bucket** or an **Ink Bottle**, depending on where you clicked.*

▷ Click the shape onto which you want to apply the copied fill/stroke.

I- Erasing a shape

▷ Select the **Eraser** tool  or press the **E** key.

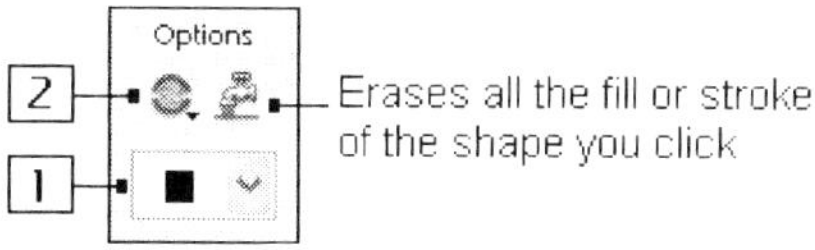

1 Select a type of eraser.

2 Select the erasing mode:

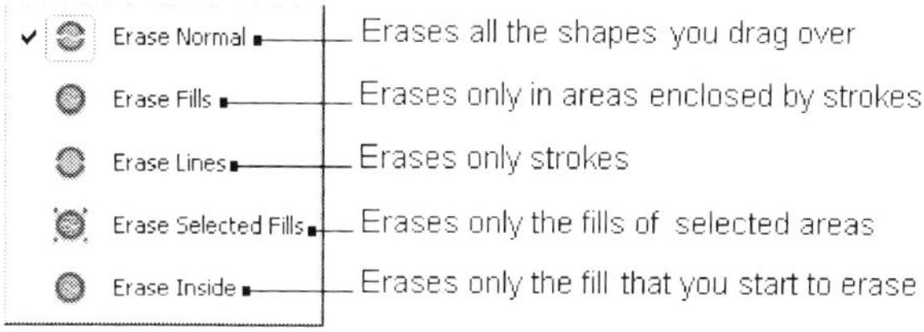

▷ Drag over the drawing to erase.

⇨ *A double-click on the **Eraser** tool erases the entire contents of the stage.*

J- Transforming a stroke into a fill

You can apply a gradient or bitmap fill to a line.

▷ Select the stroke.

▷ **Modify - Shape - Convert Lines to Fills**

K-Expanding or contracting a shape's fill

▷ Select the fill in question.

▷ **Modify - Shape - Expand Fill**

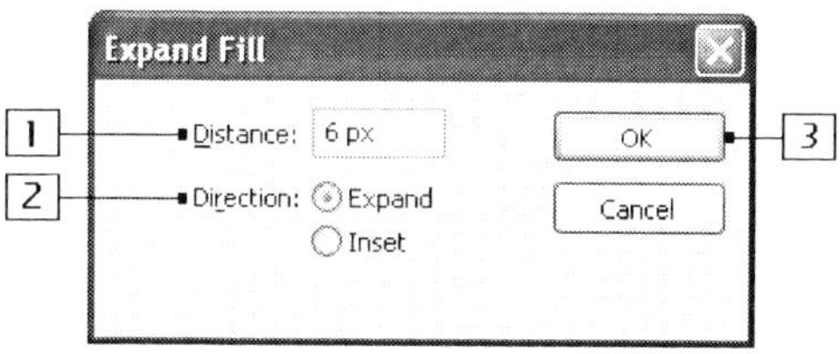

1 Give the value in pixels.

2 Choose **Expand** to stretch the fill outwards, or **Inset** to contract it inwards.

3 Click to confirm.

L- Softening the edges of a fill

This technique applies different fills over a specific distance, to create an impression of progressive transparency to the fill.

▷ Select the fill in question.

▷ **Modify - Shape - Soften Fill Edges**

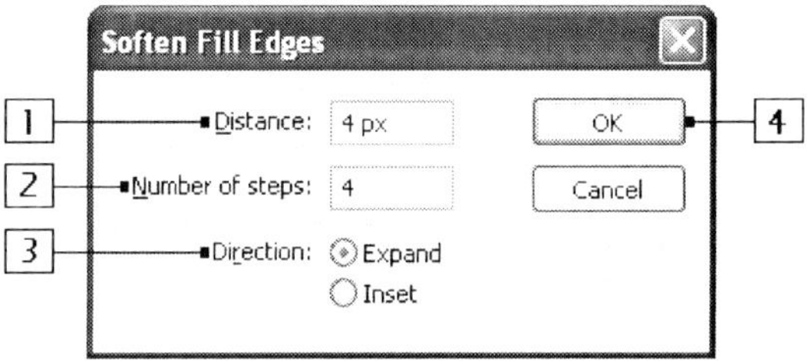

1 Enter the distance in pixels over which the transition should appear.

2 Choose the number of steps or curves through which the gradient must pass.

3 Choose **Expand** to extend the fill outwards, or **Inset** to soften the edges without resizing the fill.

4 Click to confirm.

⇨ *Softening the edges of fills increases the movie file size.*

2.3 Colours and gradients

A- Selecting a stroke or fill colour

Using the Tools panel

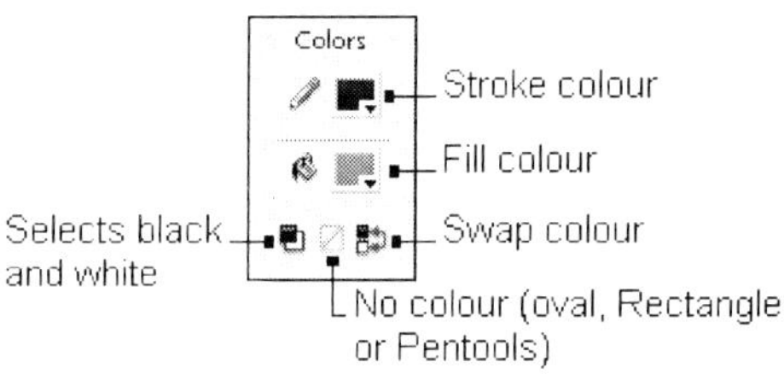

▷ Click the **Stroke Color** button or **Fill Color** button to display a pop-up colour palette:

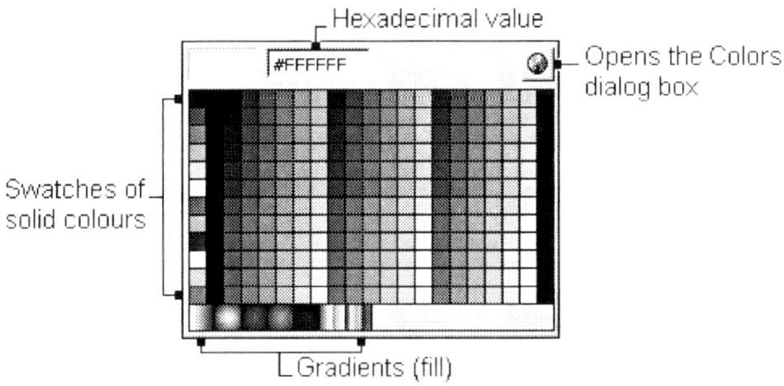

▷ Click a colour to select it.

Using the Colors dialog box

▷ Click the button or the button on the **Tools** panel and click the button.

On a PC

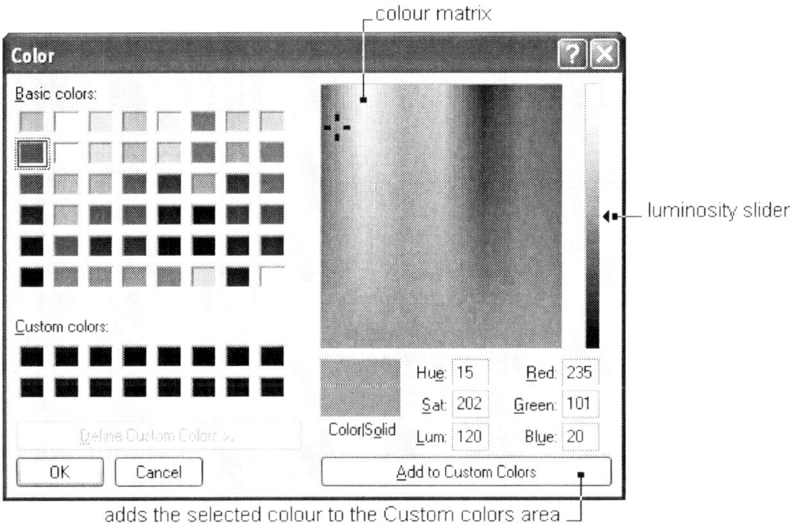

▷ Click one of the **Basic colors** or **Custom colors**.
or
Click the colour space (drag the lightness slider to change the luminosity).
or
Set the HSL or RGB components of the colour.

▷ Click **OK** to confirm.

On a Mac

▷ Click the **Color Wheel** button  or the **Color Palettes** button 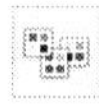 to show the colour wheel or a selection of palettes.

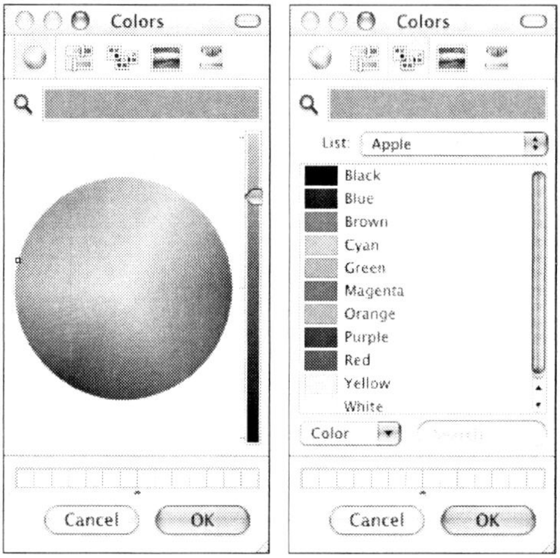

▷ Click in the colour space or on a colour in a palette, depending on the display mode.

▷ Click **OK**.

Using the Color Mixer

▷ **Window**
Design Panels
Color Mixer ⇧ Shift F9

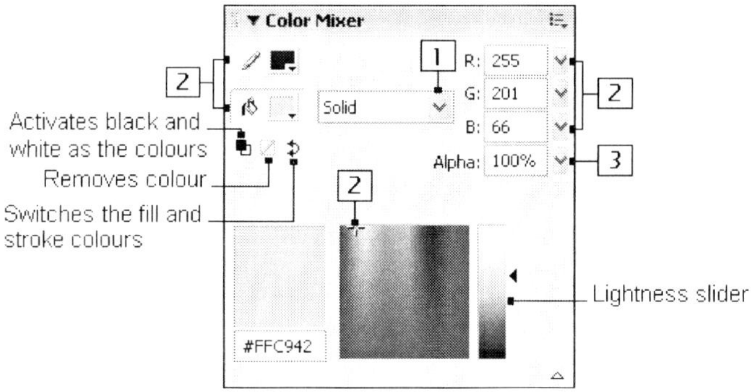

1 Select **Solid** as the **Fill style** (the **None** style applies a transparent stroke or fill).

2 Choose the type of colour you want to modify (**Stroke color** and/or **Fill color**) and click the 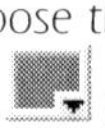 button to select the colour,
or click the colour space, dragging the lightness slider if necessary,
or set the colour's RGB components.

3 To change the colour's transparency, change its **Alpha** value (100% for an opaque colour, 0% for perfect transparency).

Using the Color Swatches panel

▷ **Window**
Design Panels
Color Swatches

Ctrl F9 (PC)
⌘ F9 (Mac)

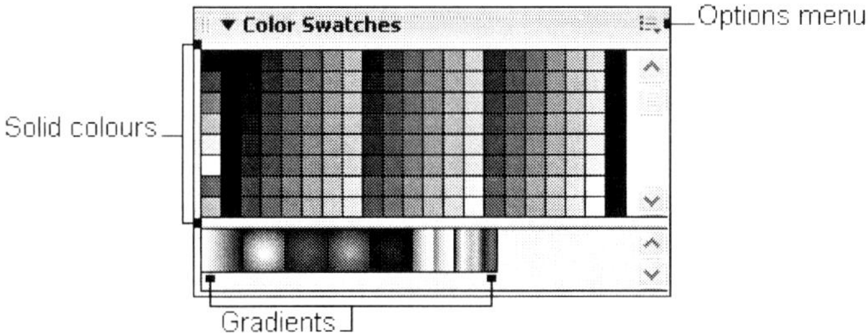

▷ Click the **Stroke Color** or **Fill Color** button then click the swatch for the colour or gradient you want to use.

⇨ *You can sort swatch palettes by groups of hues by activating the* ***Sort by Color*** *option in the* ***Options*** *menu.*

Using the Property inspector

▷ Select the **Stroke Color** or **Fill Color**:

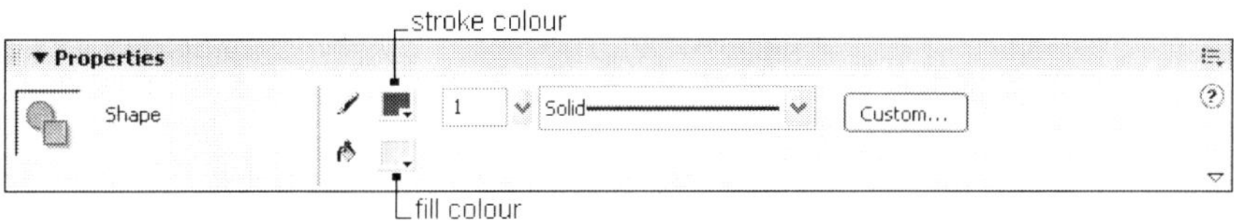

B - Creating a gradient

▷ Display the **Color Mixer** panel.

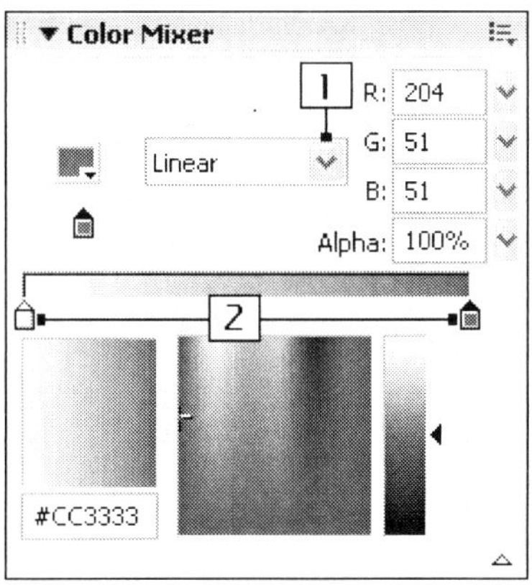

1 Select the type of gradient: **Linear** or **Radial**.

2 Set the colours for the gradient: click one of the pointers underneath the gradient definition bar and choose a colour. You can add a gradient pointer by clicking under the gradient definition bar and selecting a colour. You can modify the gradient by sliding the pointers. To delete a pointer, drag it downwards.

▷ To save a gradient, open the **Color Mixer** panel's **Options** menu  and choose **Add Swatch**.

*This adds the swatch to the **Color Swatches** panel.*

⇨ *To edit an existing gradient, select it in the **Color Swatches** panel, then make your changes in the **Color Mixer** panel.*

C - Applying a gradient to one or more shapes

▷ Create the gradient in the **Color Mixer** panel or select a gradient in the **Color Swatches** panel.

▷ Select the  tool.

▷ To ensure that the entire gradient is applied to each shape, make sure that the  button is not active in the **Options** area of the **Tools** panel.

▷ Click the shape or shapes where you want to apply the gradient.

Here, the gradient is not locked, so it appears in its entirety in each shape:

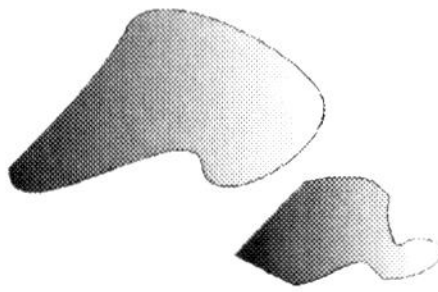

Here, the gradient was locked before filling the uppermost shape; the gradient extends over both shapes:

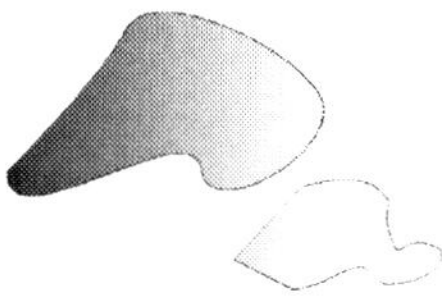

D - Changing a gradient's settings

▷ Select the **Fill Transform** tool .

▷ Click the shape containing a gradient.

▷ Drag one of the gradient's handles:

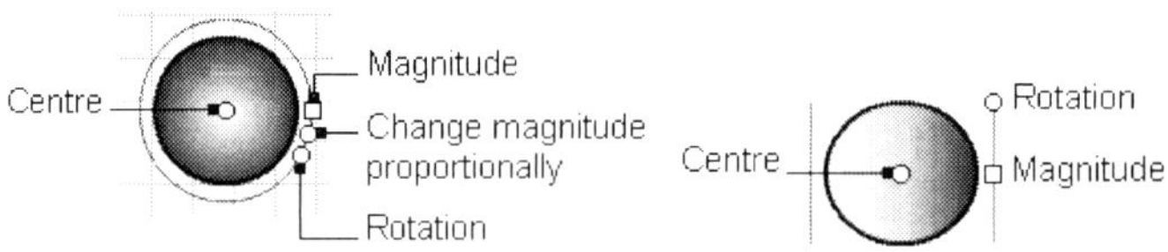

Radial gradient *Linear gradient*

E- Creating a colour set

Each Flash document has its own palette of colours that appears in the ***Color Swatches*** *panel. This panel contains by default 216 colours intended for Web use. You can create your own set of colours to use in other Flash documents, as well as in other programs such as Fireworks or Adobe Photoshop.*

▷ Display the **Color Swatches** panel.

▷ Click the **Clear Colors** option in the **Options** menu to remove the active swatches.

All the colours are removed, except black and white.

▷ To add a colour to the swatches, define the colour or gradient in the **Color Mixer**, then click the **Color Swatches** panel.

▷ To duplicate a colour from the swatches, click it in the **Color Swatches** panel, open the **Options** menu and choose **Duplicate Swatch**.

▷ To remove a colour from the swatches, click it, open the **Options** menu and choose **Delete Swatch**.

▷ Once your colour set is complete, save it using the **Save Colors** command in the **Options** menu.

Under Windows, the created file carries a .clr file extension.

⇨ *The* ***Save as Default*** *option in the* ***Options*** *menu defines the current set as the default set.*

⇨ *To use a previously-created set of colours, use the* ***Add Colors*** *or* ***Replace Colors*** *option in the* ***Options*** *menu to respectively complement the current set or replace it by the one you are importing.*

⇨ *To retrieve the colour set supplied by default, use the* ***Load Default Colors*** *option from the* ***Options*** *menu.*

3.1 Text

A-Creating a text block on the stage

There are three types of text block:

- *Static text blocks contain fixed text that the final user cannot edit.*
- *Dynamic text blocks have variable content and can be updated using hyperlinks or ActionScript code.*
- *Input text blocks allow the final user to edit text (for example, for a password).*

▷ Select the **Text** tool or press the **T** key.

▷ Select the type of text block in the **Text type** pop-up menu in the Property inspector.

▷ Click on the stage where you want to create the text block.

▷ Enter your text. If necessary, use the Enter key to create a new paragraph.

▷ With **static** text, the block is of variable size. It expands as you enter the text. To fix the width of the block, drag its handle. Once the text reaches the edge of the block, it will drop down to a new line.

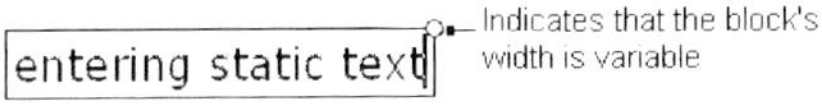

Block of fixed width

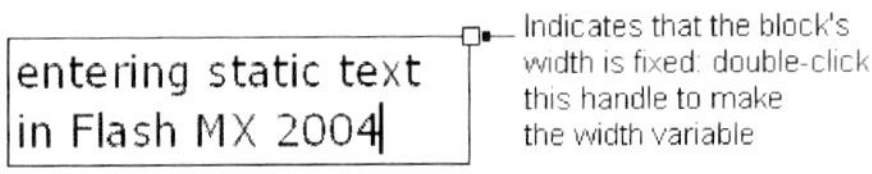

Block of fixed width

▷ For **dynamic** or **input** text, the block is of fixed width. When the text reaches the edge of the block, it will drop down to the next line as you keep typing. To change the width and/or height of the block, drag the square handle. To lock the size of the block, hold down ⇧Shift and double-click the handle. Locking the block makes scroll bars appear when the text is too long.

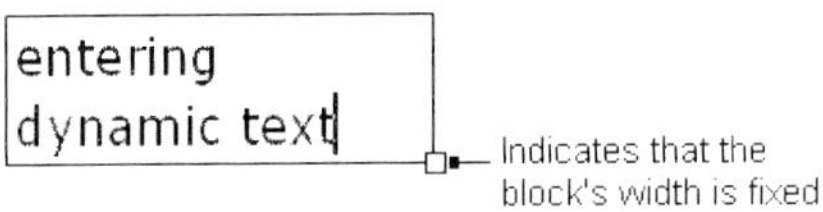

Block of fixed width

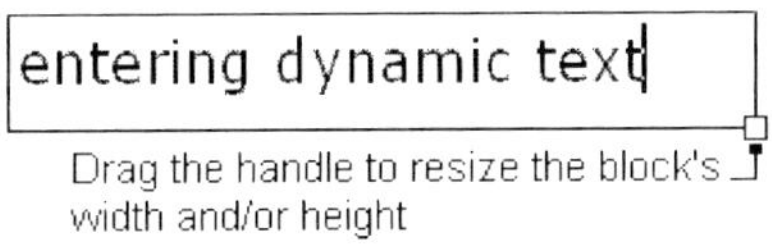

Fixed width block resized

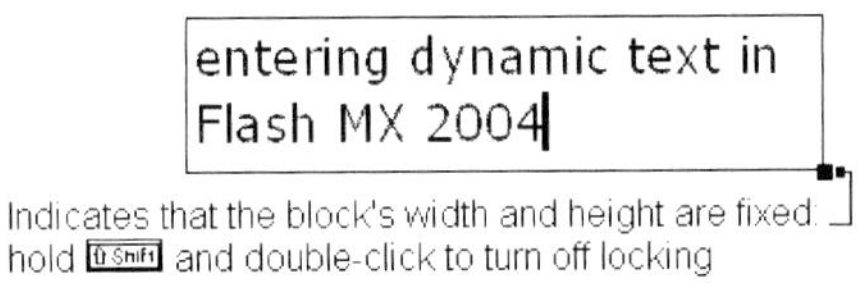

Block of locked width and height

▷ Click outside the text bock to confirm.

⇨ *To change the text in a block, select the **Text** tool or the tool and, depending on the tool, click or double-click the text block, then make the required changes.*

⇨ *It is a good idea to use the **Subselection** tool to select a text block, as there is no risk of selecting the text within it.*

⇨ *The **Text - Scrollable** command can also be used to lock the size of a block of dynamic text and to display scroll bars if the text is too long.*

B - Formatting characters

▷ Select the text or text block.

*Select a word with a double-click using the **Text** tool.*

▷ Display the Property inspector.

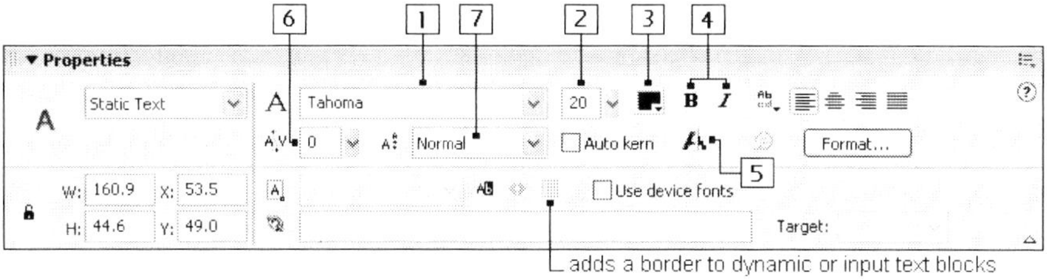

1 Select the required font.

2 Select a character size.

3 Select a colour for the characters.

4 If necessary, apply **Bold** and **Italic** styles.

5 If required, activate anti-aliasing to improve the legibility of small characters. This feature is only managed by the end user if he or she is using Flash Player 7 or later.

6 You can change the spacing between characters. If you tick the **Auto kern** option, Flash applies specific kerning to each pair of characters.

7 To display a character in subscript or superscript, select the appropriate option.

⇨ *Spacing can also be changed with keyboard shortcuts:*

Ctrl Alt → (PC)	⌘ ⌥ → (Mac)	*To increase the spacing.*
Ctrl Alt ← (PC)	⌘ ⌥ ← (Mac)	*To decrease the spacing.*
Ctrl Alt ↑ (PC)	⌘ ⌥ ↑ (Mac)	*To return to the default spacing of 0.*

C - Formatting paragraphs

▷ Display the Property inspector.

▷ Select the paragraph or text block concerned. If only one paragraph is concerned, click in that paragraph.

▷ To define the alignment, click one of these icons in the Property inspector:

Left align	Centre
Right align	Justify

▷ To change the indent, the line spacing or the paragraph margins, click the **Format** button on the Property inspector:

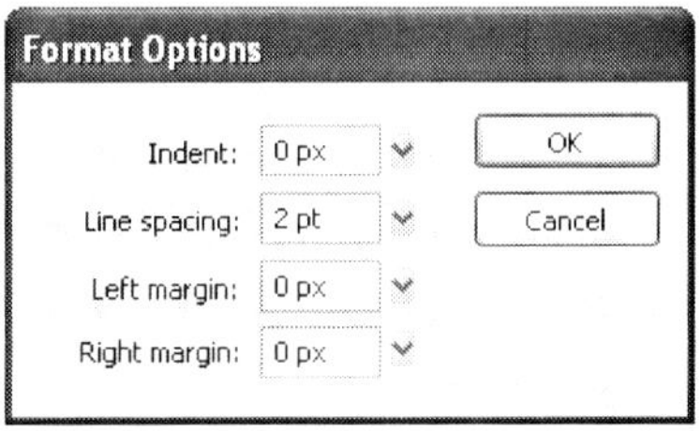

▷ If you want static text to be aligned vertically, click the button and choose **Vertical, Left to Right** or **Vertical, Right to Left**. Next, click one of the alignment icons to align the text at the top of the block, centre it between the top and bottom, align it at the bottom of the block or justify it between the top and bottom. Click the **Rotation** button to change the orientation.

Vertical alignment *From left to right* *After rotation, the text is aligned at the top of the block*

D - Applying the properties of one text block onto another

▷ Select the target text block.

▷ Select the **Eyedropper** tool then click the source text block.

E - Breaking text apart

This enables you to manipulate each character like a graphic symbol.

▷ Select the text block concerned.

▷ **Modify**
Break Apart

Ctrl **B** (PC)
⌘ **B** (Mac)

You can select each character independently from the others and convert it into an editable shape. To do this, apply this command again to the character.

⇨ *Only True Type fonts and/or PostScript fonts on a Mac can be broken apart.*

F- Defining properties for each type of text block

The available properties differ depending on the type of text block (static, dynamic or input).

Static text

▷ Tick the **Use device fonts** option if you want to be sure that the text is correctly displayed even if the end user's system does not have that font.

When you publish the movie, the vector fonts of static text are exported. You can ask Flash to use device fonts instead, reducing the file size and improving the sharpness of small fonts. Flash uses three device fonts: _serif (equivalent of Times New Roman), _typewriter (equivalent of Courier), and _sans (equivalent of Helvetica or Arial). When the movie plays, Flash uses the first font it finds on the user's system. This means that the text's appearance may differ between platforms.

▷ If you want to allow the end user to select the text block, click the **Selectable** button.

⇨ *You can also set which replacement fonts to use if one of the movie's fonts is not available on the end user's system (cf. next heading).*

Dynamic text

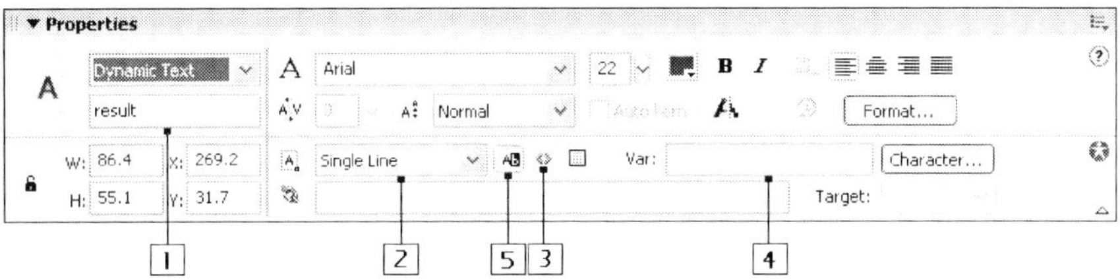

[1] Indicate the **Instance Name**.

[2] Choose how the text is laid out in the text block:

Single Line	Whatever its length, the text appears on a single line.
Multiline	The text may appear on several lines, depending on its length.
Multiline no wrap	The text may appear on several lines, providing that manual line breaks have been inserted.

[3] Click this button if you want to apply HTML tags for the various attributes (colour, size, style etc.) automatically during exportation.

[4] Enter a name for the variable.

[5] Make the text selectable if required.

When you publish the movie, Flash saves only the names of the fonts used and when it plays the movie, it looks for those fonts, or their equivalent, on the user's computer. If you want the display to be the same as the original, you can always export the font outlines, which increases the file size as a result.

▷ To do this, click the **Character** button.

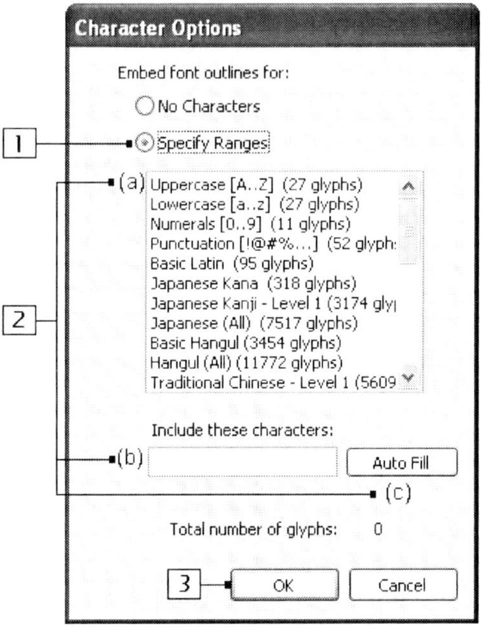

1 Activate this option.

2 Choose the type of character you want to integrate (a) or select the required characters (b) or click this button (c) to include each character from the selected text.

3 Click to confirm.

You can attach a hyperlink to a block of static or dynamic text (cf. point H in this chapter).

Input text

▷ If you want the text in the block to appear as asterisks as it is typed in, select the **Password** option in the **Line type** pop-up menu.

▷ Specify the **Maximum characters** that can be entered in the block.

⇨ *You also have access to the same properties as for dynamic text.*

G-Setting replacement fonts

These fonts are used when a font is not integrated in a movie and the font is not available on the end user's system.

▷ **Edit** (PC)/**Flash** (Mac)
Font Mapping

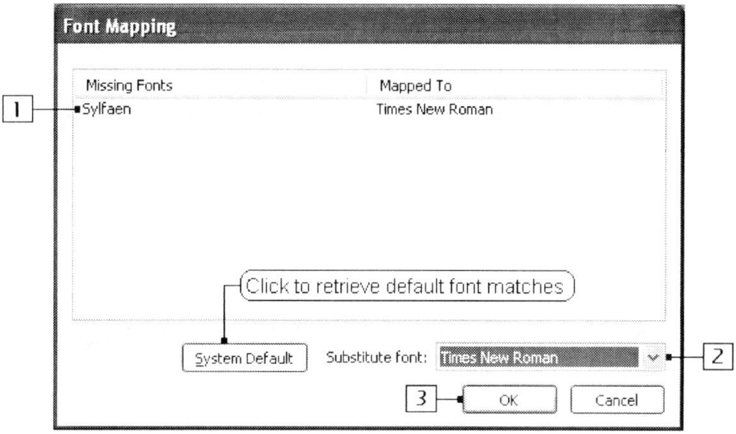

1 Select one of the missing fonts.

2 Select a replacement font.

3 Click to confirm.

H-Attaching a hyperlink to a static or dynamic text block

▷ Select the text block concerned.

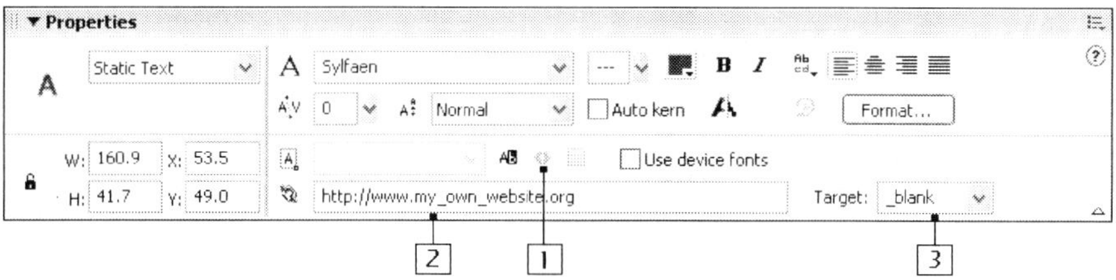

1 For dynamic text, activate this option.

2 Enter the URL address. You can enter an e-mail address in the form of mailto:address@server.com

3 Define the window or frame into which the web page should load:

_blank	Loads the page into a new window.
_parent	Loads the page into the parent window or frame.
_self	Loads the page into the active window or frame.
_top	Loads the page into the top level window or frame.

3.2 Importing images

A- Import formats

Extension	File type
.eps .ai .pdf	Adobe Illustrator, version 6 and higher
.dxf	AutoCad DXF
.bmp	Bitmap (with QuickTime for Macintosh)
.gif	GIF and animated GIF
.jpg	JPEG
.png	PNG
.swf	Flash movie
.wmf	Windows metafile
.fh7 to .fh11	FreeHand, version 7 and higher

▷ If QuickTime 4 or higher is installed, you can also import the following formats:

Extension	File type
.psd	Photoshop
.tga	Targa
.tif	TIFF
.pct .pic	PICT
.sgi	Silicon Graphics Image
.qtif	QuickTime Image
.pntg	MacPaint

B- Importing one or several files

▷ To import the file into the Library, use **File - Import - Import to Library**.

To import the file onto the stage and into the Library, click the layer in question and use:

File
Import
Import to Stage

Ctrl **R** (PC)
⌘ **R** (Mac)

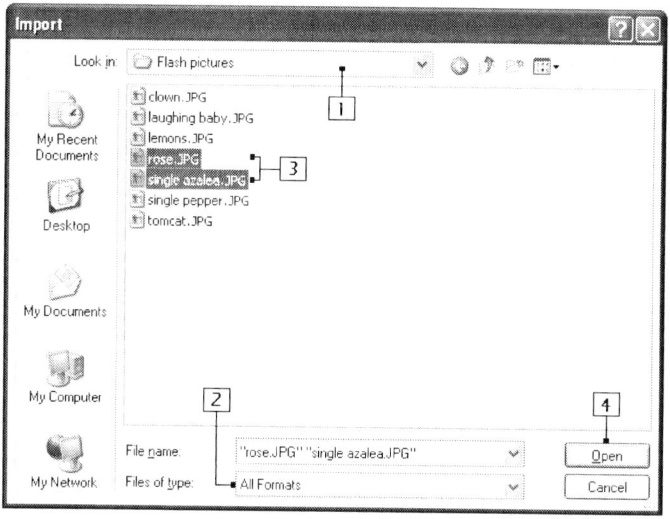

1 Go to the folder containing the file you want to import.

2 Select the file format (Bitmap, GIF, JPEG, PICT, MacPaint etc.).

3 Select the file or files (use the Ctrl or ⇧ Shift keys for multiple selections).

4 Import the files.

On a Mac, choose a file type in the ***Enable*** *list if necessary, browse in the file explorer in the dialog box, click the file (⌘-click for multiple selections) and click the* ***Import*** *button.*

Importing an Illustrator, EPS or PDF file

When you import an Illustrator file (version 6 or higher), the following dialog box appears:

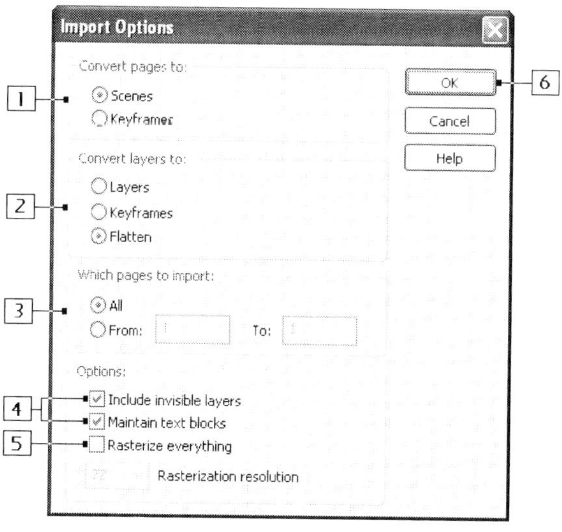

TEXT, IMAGES, SOUND & VIDEO

1 Indicate whether each page in the file must be imported as a scene or as a keyframe.

2 Indicate whether each layer in the file must be imported as a layer, a keyframe or if the layers should be flattened before importing.

3 Specify which pages to import.

4 Indicate whether to include hidden layers or to convert text blocks (the text can then be modified in Flash).

5 Tick this option to convert everything into bitmap and indicate the conversion resolution (in dots per inch): **72** is suitable for a screen use document and for professional printing, choose **300**.

6 Click to confirm.

If the file contains fonts that are unavailable on your computer, a dialog box will appear.

▷ Click the **Choose Substitute** button to choose an existing font, or **Use Default** to replace it with the standard replacement font.

⇨ *To edit the elements of an imported file separately, you must ungroup them (cf. chapter 4.2 - H - Ungrouping a group of objects).*

C - Defining properties for a bitmap image

This feature allows you to define the compression mode used for the image, in order to lighten the file size.

▷ Select the image in the Library.

▷ Open the **Options** menu then choose the **Properties** option or click the icon at the bottom of the **Library** panel or double-click the image icon.

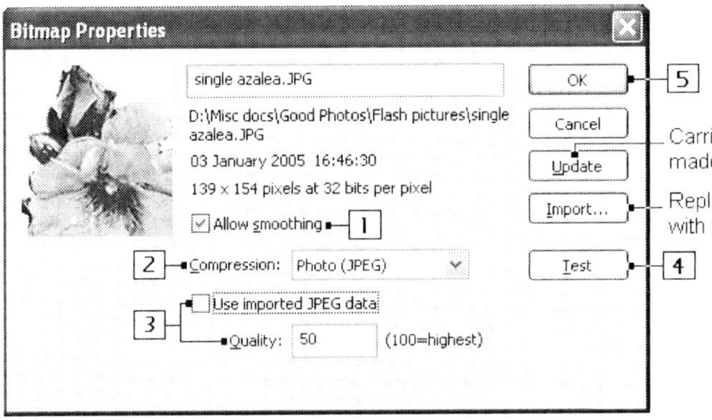

1 Tick this option to smooth the image outlines.

2 Define the compression mode:

Photo (JPEG)	Generally used for photos or pictures using a large number of colours.
(Lossless (PNG/GIF)	The **PNG** format preserves transparency effects (the file is larger than with **JPEG** format); **GIF** format is used when a minimum of colours is required (maximum 256 colours).

3 To change the compression settings, deactivate this check box and give the level of quality to apply (between 0 and 100).

4 To compare the size of the original file with that of the compressed file, click this button.

5 Click to confirm.

D - Modifying a bitmap image

▷ Select the image in the Library.

▷ Open the **Options** menu then choose **Edit with**.

▷ Select the application you want to use.

▷ Make your changes and then save the file.

The file will be automatically updated in Flash.

⇨ *If the original file has been modified independently of Flash, use the **Update** button in the **Bitmap Properties** dialog box to carry the changes over into Flash.*

⇨ *If you make your changes in Fireworks, you will be able to choose between changing the source file (.png) or the bitmap file (.bmp). To update into Flash, use **File - Update**.*

E - Converting a bitmap image into a vector graphic

This feature helps reduce the file size, but cannot be applied to all bitmaps.

▷ On the stage, select the bitmap image you want to convert.

▷ **Modify - Bitmap - Trace Bitmap**

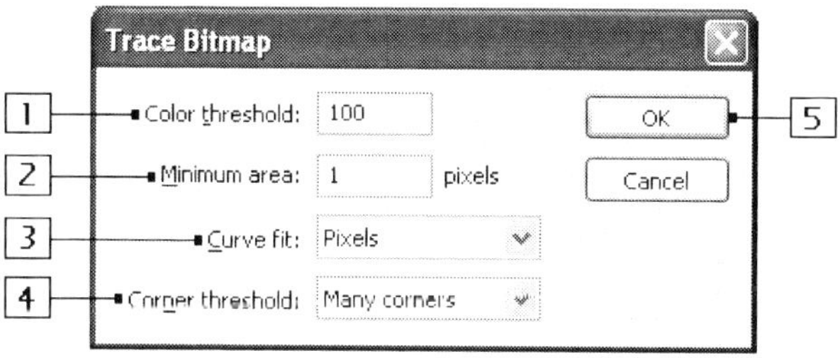

1 The value indicated here determines how many colours will be preserved. Flash compares the pixels and when the colour difference is lower than the threshold, it considers them to be the same colour. The higher the threshold, the lower the number of colours.

2 Enter the number of surrounding pixels that Flash must consider when it assigns a colour to a pixel.

3 Select how smoothly Flash should draw outlines (the **Very Smooth** option reduces the file size).

4 Specify whether Flash should keep sharp edges or smooth them out (the **Few Corners** option reduces the file size).

5 Click to confirm.

3.3 Sound and video

A - Import formats

The following **audio** formats can be imported into Flash MX 2004:

	PC	Mac
.mp3	Yes	Yes
.wav	Yes	No
.aiff	No	Yes

From QuickTime 4 onwards, you can import these formats:

	PC	Mac
Sound Designer II	No	Yes
Sun AU	Yes	Yes
System 7 Sounds	No	Yes
.wav	Yes	Yes

From QuickTime 4 onwards and version 7 of DirectX, you can import these video formats:

.mpg, .mpeg	Motion Picture Experts Group
.avi	Audio Video Interleaved
.dv	Digital Video
.mov	QuickTime
.wmv	Windows Media
.asf	Windows Media

⇨ *You should install the latest version of QuickTime for PC and Mac, and DirectX for PC.*

B - Importing a sound into a movie

▷ Import the audio file into the Library:

File
Import
Import to Library

Select the file(s) you want to import and click **Open** (PC) or **Import to Library** (Mac).

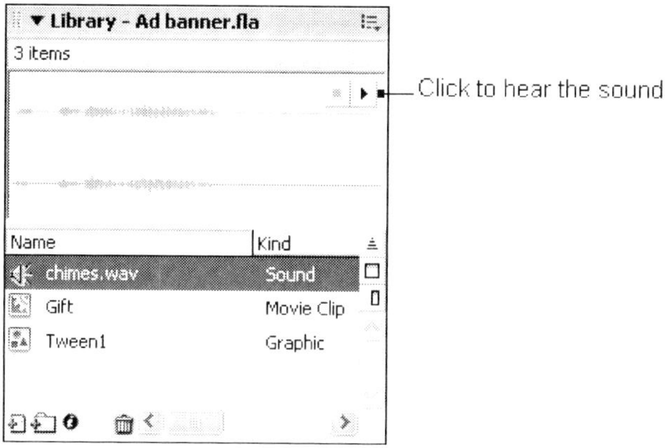

- ▷ To insert the sound into the movie, select an empty layer and drag the sound from the Library onto the stage.
- ▷ Click the sound's first frame then open the **Sync** pop-up menu on the Property inspector and choose how the sound should play:

Event The sound plays when an event occurs (a click on the button for example); it is played independently and continues even when the movie stops. If the event occurs again while the sound is still playing, for example if the user clicks the button again, a new occurrence of the sound will start.

Start Similar to the **Event** option, but if the event occurs again, the sound stops before restarting.

Stop Use to stop playing a sound.

Stream The sound is played with streaming; if some images in the movie cannot be displayed quickly enough, they will be ignored so as not to perturb the synchronisation between sound and image. If the animations stops, the sound stops automatically.

- ▷ In the pop-up menu next to that, choose **Loop** if you want the sound to play over and over or **Repeat** to define how many times the sound should play.
- ▷ If necessary, modify the sound's audio properties (cf. below).

⇨ *It is a good idea to place only one sound per layer.*

C - Modifying a sound's audio properties

- ▷ Select the sound in the Library.
- ▷ Open the **Options** menu and choose the **Properties** option or click the icon at the bottom of the **Library** panel or double-click the sound file's icon.

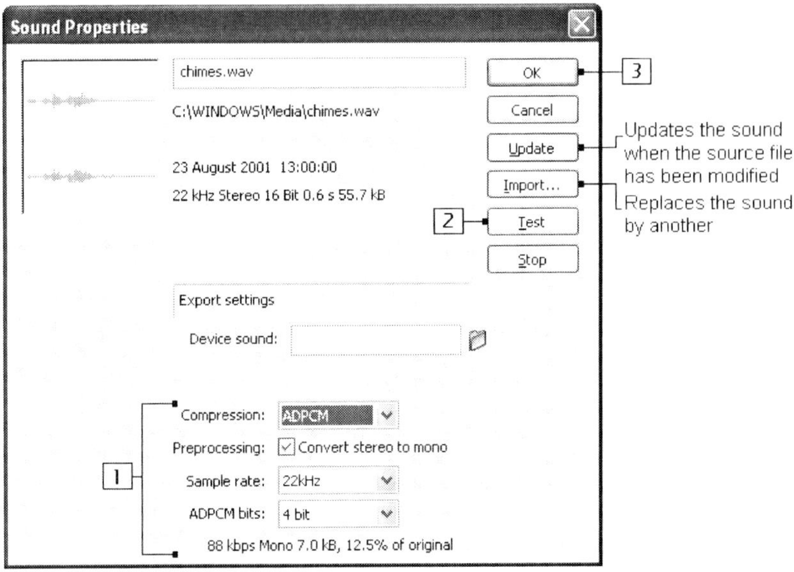

1 Set a compression mode and its associated settings (which vary from one mode to another):

Default Applies the compression parameters defined in the **Publish Settings** dialog box.

ADPCM This compression mode is used for 8-bit or 16-bit sound files or short sounds. Tick the **Preprocessing** check box if you want to convert to mono. Choose a **Sample rate** (**5kHz**, **11kHz**, **22kHz** or **44kHz**): the lower the rate, the smaller the file size, but this will affect the quality (the 22kHz rate is often used for the Web; 44kHz is CD quality sound, but if sound quality is not a priority, you can sue 5 or 11kHz). In the **ADPCM bits** pop-up menu, choose the number of bits that will play at the chosen sample rate (**2**, **3**, **4** or **5** bits) to define the sound bit rate. The lower the bit rate, the more the sound is affected.

MP3 This compression mode is often used for background music. Choose a **Bit rate**; the 16 Kbits/s default is suitable for most uses. If the value is lower than 20 Kbits/s, the **Preprocessing** option will be unavailable. If it is available, tick its check box if you want to convert to mono. In the **Quality** field, choose a compression rate (**Fast**, **Medium** or **Best**): the higher the speed, the lower the sound quality.

Raw Select this option to prevent sound compression. Tick the **Preprocessing** check box if you want to convert to mono. Give a **Sample rate**.

Speech Select this option for spoken word files. A **Sample rate** of 5kHz or 11kHz is usually sufficient for this type of sound.

2 Click this button to check the sound after compression.

3 Click to confirm.

D-Applying an effect to a sound

▷ In the Timeline, click the frame containing the sound.

▷ Display the Property inspector.

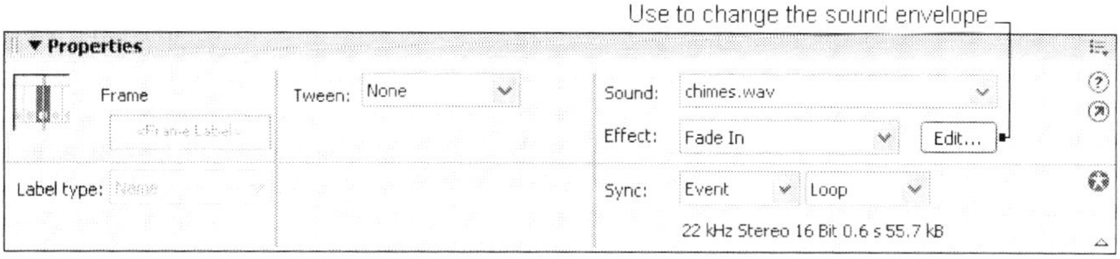

▷ Select the **Effect** you want to apply to the sound:

Left Channel/ Right Channel	Plays the sound only in the specified channel.
Fade Right to Left/ Fade Left to Right	The sound moves from one channel to the other.
Fade In	The volume increases progressively.
Fade Out	The volume decreases progressively.
Custom	This option lets you control the fade in and fade out points yourself (cf. Modifying sound volume).

⇨ *The effect can also be applied to a Library sound. In this case, it will apply to every occurrence of that sound.*

E- Modifying sound volume

▷ On the Timeline, click a frame containing sound.

▷ Click the **Edit** button on the Property inspector.

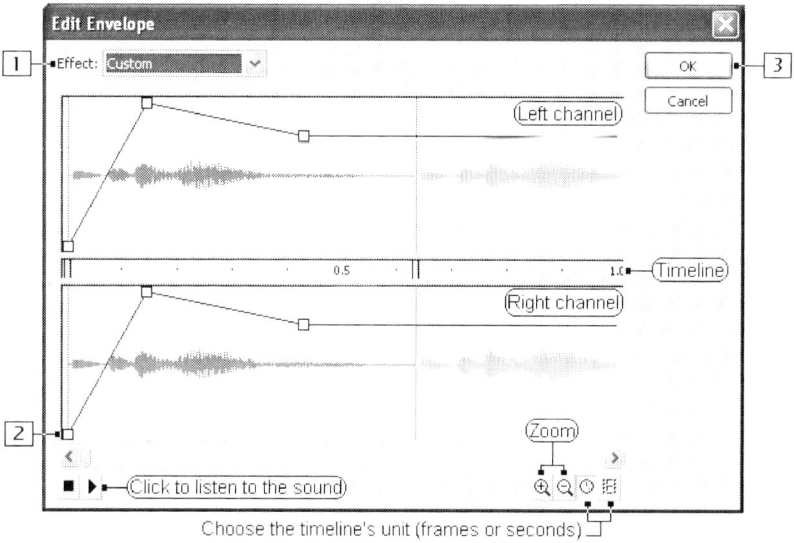

TEXT, IMAGES, SOUND & VIDEO

1 If necessary, modify the applied effect (cf. previous heading).

2 To modify the sound envelope, drag each handle. To create an envelope handle, click the envelope line. To delete a handle, drag it outside the window.

3 Once you are happy with the settings, click to confirm.

F - Importing a video into a movie

A wizard helps you import a video file, through a series of steps: creating clips from a video if necessary, choosing a compression profile, settings advanced parameters and importing.

▷ To import a video onto the Stage:

File
Import
Import to Stage

Ctrl **R** (PC)
⌘ **R** (Mac)

To import a video into the Library, use the **File - Import - Import to Library** command.

▷ Select the video file you want to import and click **Open**.

If you import a QuickTime or AVI video, this dialog box appears:

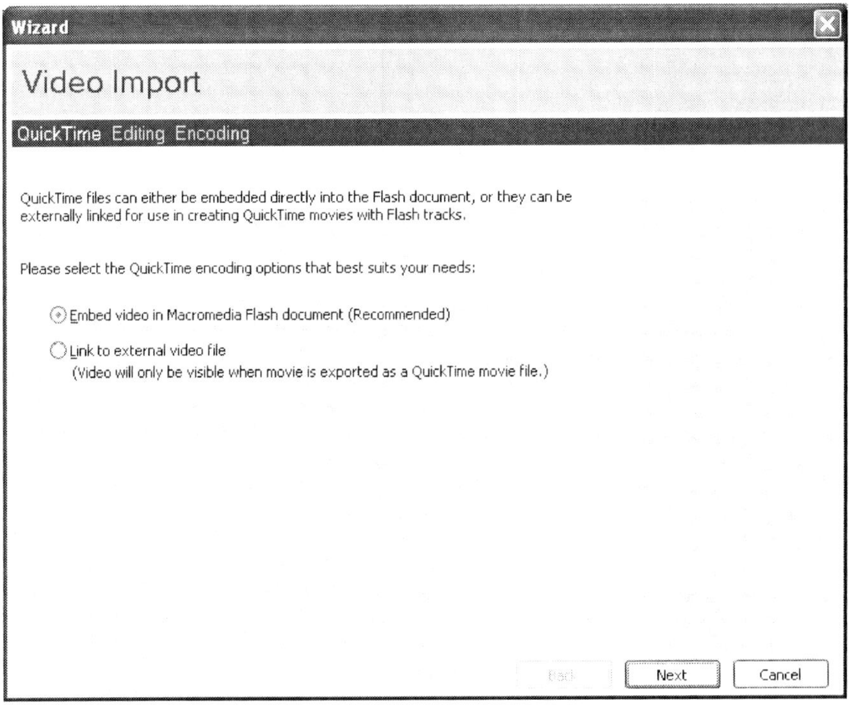

If you choose the second option, the video will not be embedded into the movie, but a link will be made with the corresponding video file. In this case, the Flash file must be published in QuickTime format.

▷ Click **Next**.

*The **Video Import** wizard dialog box appears on the screen.*

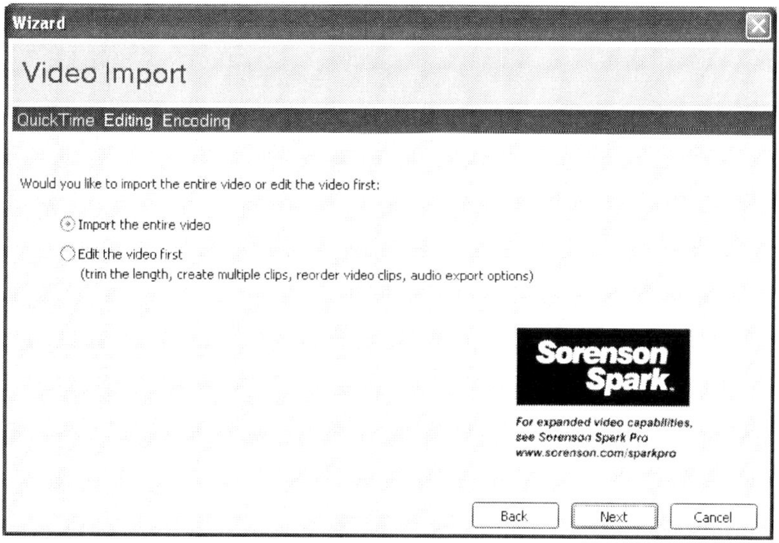

The Sorensen Spark codec manages compressing the video in Flash and decompressing it as it plays.

Creating one or more clips from a video

▷ Select the **Edit the video first** option and click **Next**.

*The **Editing** step of the **Video Import** wizard opens in the dialog box.*

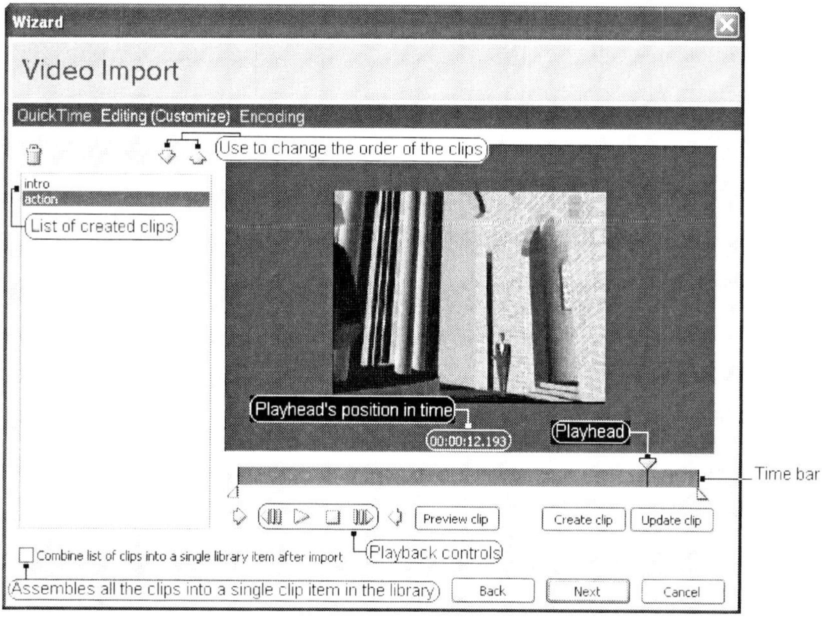

▷ Drag the triangular sliders at each end of the time bar or place the playhead at the place where the clip should start and click the button, then place the playhead at the place where the clip should finish and click the button.

▷ Click the **Create clip** button.

The clip you create is added in the left pane of the window.

▷ If necessary, modify the clip's name and confirm with Enter.

▷ Repeat these actions if necessary to create other clips from the same video.

⇨ *To change the length of a clip, select it in the list, move the sliders on the time bar and click the **Update clip** button.*

Choosing or creating a compression profile

▷ Click **Next**.

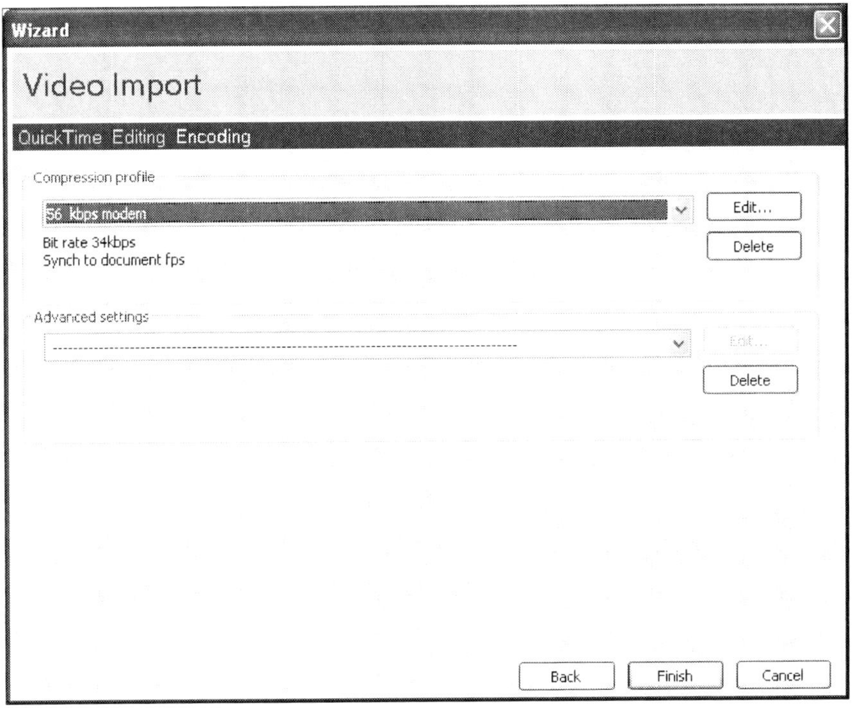

▷ Select a **Compression profile** depending on the file size and the speed of the modem that will be used during play: for example, **56 kbps modem** is equivalent to a classic analog modem, with a transfer rate of 3 to 4 kb/s while **DSL/Cable 512kbps** is equivalent in speed to a classic ADSL connection with a transfer rate of 60 kb/s.

If there is no suitable profile, click the **Create new profile** option.

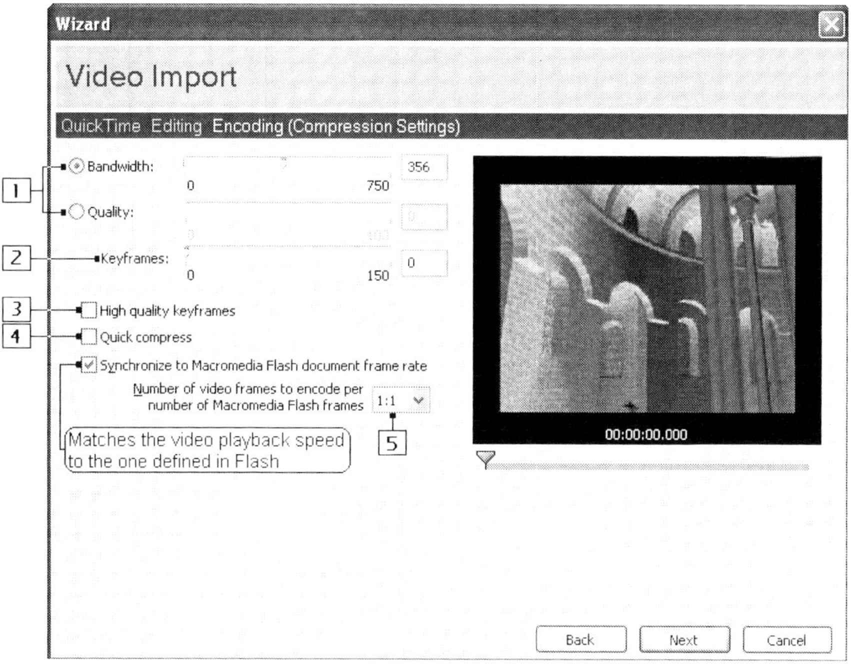

1 Choose a video optimisation criterion (the bandwidth is the theoretical speed of your Internet connection) and drag the slider concerned to modify the value, using the preview box to help you.

2 Define the interval used for uncompressed frames.

3 If you chose the **Bandwidth** option, activate this option to minimise quality problems on keyframes.

4 Tick this option to reduce compression time. This choice may affect the quality.

5 Define the number of frames imported in relation to the number of frames in the movie. For example, with a value of **1:2**, one video frame will be imported for two frames of the movie. This setting is linked to how smoothly the video plays

▷ Click **Next**.

▷ Enter a **Name** for the profile you created and a **Description**, if you wish.

▷ Click **Next**.

*The profile name appears in the **Compression profile** field.*

Setting advanced options

These settings concern colour, frame sizes, and how the video will be imported.

▷ Open the **Advanced settings** pop-up menu and choose **Create new profile**.

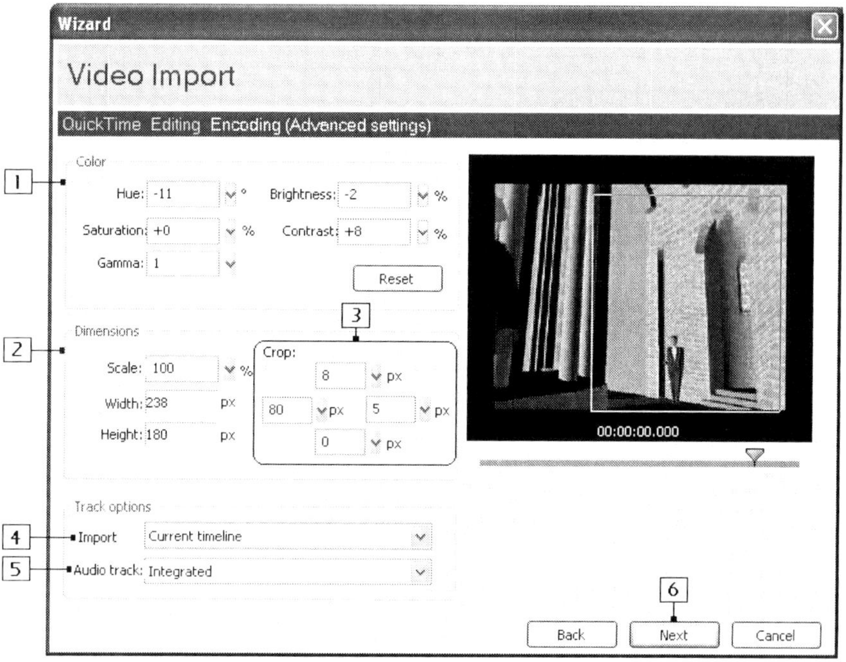

1 If necessary, modify these options to correct the colours in the video. The **Gamma** option affects the global luminosity level of the frames.

2 If necessary, resize the frames proportionally. The size appears in the **Width** and **Height** boxes.

3 Use these fields if you want to crop the frame edges.

4 Specify the importation method to be used:

Current timeline	This imports the video as a video item in the current Timeline. This method allows you to browse through the video within the active Timeline, but you cannot add any special effects to it.
Movie clip	This imports the video as a clip in the first frame of the Timeline. To browse through the frames, you will need to open the clip Timeline. With this method, you can add special effects.
Graphic symbol	This imports the video as a graphic symbol in the active Timeline. With this method, you can browse through the video within the active Timeline and add special effects.

5 If necessary, indicate whether the audio track should be included in the video file, imported separately, or not imported at all.

6 Click **Next**.

▷ Give a **Name** for the settings and a **Description**, if you wish, then click **Next**.

Finalising the importation

▷ Click **Finish** to start importing the video.

A window appears to show how the importation is progressing.

If there are not enough active frames in the Timeline to contain the video, Flash will display a warning.

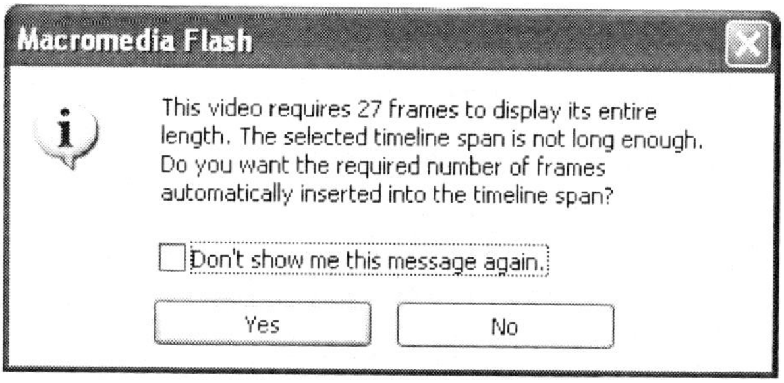

▷ Click **Yes** to increase the span of frames in the Timeline.

▷ If you imported the video into the Library, drag it onto the stage to insert it into the Timeline.

⇨ *You can apply the **Free Transform** tool to a video, to rotate it, resize it etc.*

⇨ *If you update the source video file and you want to update it in Flash, display its properties by clicking the button in the Library then click the **Update** button. The **Import** button on this dialog box can replace the selected video by another.*

4.1 Selection techniques

A- Selecting all the objects on the stage

▷ **Edit**
Select All

Ctrl **A** (PC)
⌘ **A** (Mac)

▷ To cancel your selection:
Edit
Deselect All

Ctrl Shift **A** (PC)
⌘ Shift **A** (Mac)

B- Selecting one or more objects on the stage

An object refers to any item placed on the stage, such as a shape, a text block, a picture, and so on.

▷ Select the  tool or press the **V** key.

▷ To select:

- a line, click that line. If the line has corners, double-click it to select all of it.
- a fill, click that fill.
- a complete shape (fill & stroke), double-click the shape.
- a text block, click the block.
- a picture or video, click that picture of video.

▷ To select several objects, drag around the objects you want to select, or hold down the Shift key and click each object:

The selection is represented by dotted lines. Here, the fill of the first object and the stroke of the second have been selected.

⇨ *If only one object is selected, the Property inspector displays the properties of that object:*

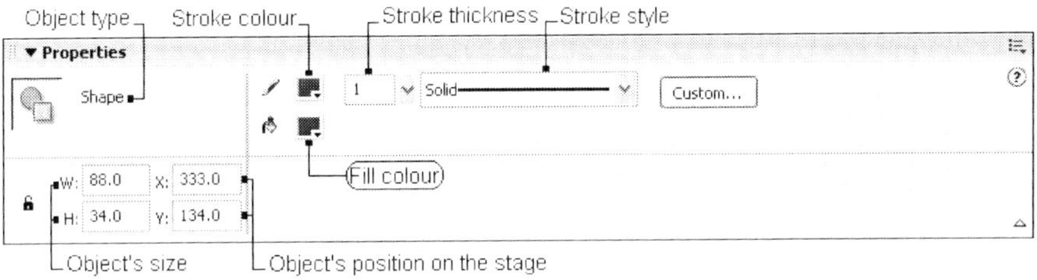

*If you select several objects, the Property inspector will display **Mixed** as the object type; only the size of the group and its position on the stage will appear.*

⇨ *If the layer containing the object is locked, selection becomes impossible.*

⇨ *If another tool is active, you can temporarily activate the tool by holding down* Ctrl *(PC) or* ⌘ *(Mac).*

⇨ *The* ⇧ Shift *key is used to add or remove other items from the current selection.*

C-Selecting with the Lasso tool

This tool is used to select a very precise area.

▷ Select the **Lasso** tool.

▷ In the **Options** area of the **Tools** panel, activate the **Polygon Mode** button if the zone you want to select can be defined with a polygon.

▷ If **Polygon Mode** is not active, drag around the area you want to select.

If you do not close the path, Flash will close it with a straight segment.

▷ If **Polygon Mode** is active, click where you wish to start the selection area and click again at each corner of the polygonal area. Close the selection area with a double-click.

⇨ *When **Polygon Mode** is not active, use the* Alt *(PC) or* ⌥ *(Mac) key to activate it temporarily.*

D-Selecting a bitmap area by its colours

▷ Break apart the bitmap image: select it on the stage and use **Modify - Break Apart**.

▷ Select the **Lasso** tool.

▷ In the **Options** area, activate the **Magic Wand** button.

▷ Set the **Magic Wand Properties** by clicking this icon.

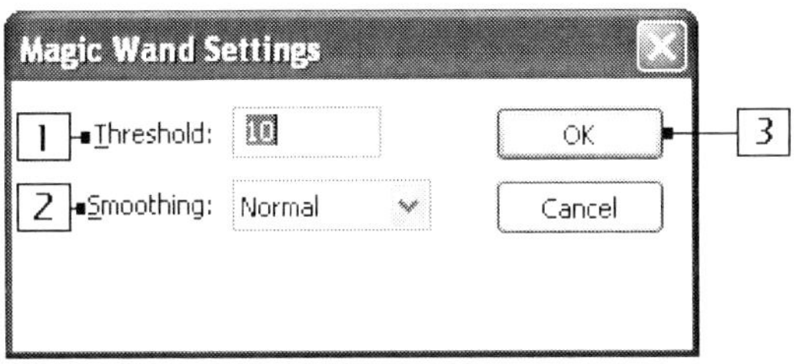

1 Indicate a value between 0 and 200 to define how closely colours must resemble each other to be selected, for example, a value of 0 selects only pixels that are exactly the same colour.

2 Indicate whether or not to smooth the selection's outlines.

3 Click to confirm.

▷ Next, click one of the pixels in the bitmap image to select all the pixels of the same (or similar) colour automatically.

You can then choose a fill colour to modify all the selected pixels.

4.2 Managing objects

A - Copying/moving objects

- Select the object(s) with the tool.
- To move objects, drag them on the stage.
- Hold down the Shift key if you need to move horizontally, vertically or diagonally.
- Hold down the Ctrl (PC) or ⌥ (Mac) key as you drag if you want to copy, and not move, objects.
- You can also move objects one pixel at a time by pressing the arrow keys. Hold down the Shift key to move by 10 pixels instead.

⇒ *If you want the objects to snap to the grid or the guides, activate the* ***Snap to Grid*** *or* ***Snap to Guides*** *command (cf. 1.3 - D - Managing guides and E - Using the grid). If objects should snap to other objects on the stage, activate the* ***Snap to Objects*** *tool or the appropriate option in the* ***View*** *menu (cf. 1.3 - Views and snapping modes).*

- Select the object(s).
- To move them:

Edit
Copy

Ctrl **C** (PC)
⌘ **C** (Mac)

- To copy them:

Edit
Cut

Ctrl **X** (PC)
⌘ **X** (Mac)

- Go to the target layer if necessary.
- **Edit**
Paste

Ctrl **V** (PC)
⌘ **V** (Mac)

⇒ *You can move all the objects from the same movie simultaneously (cf. 5.5 - Managing frames in the Timeline).*

B - Positioning an object

- Select the object.
- In the Property inspector, indicate the horizontal position in the **X** field and the vertical position in the **Y** field.
- In the **Info** panel:

Window
Design Panels
Info

Ctrl **I** (PC)
⌘ **I** (Mac)

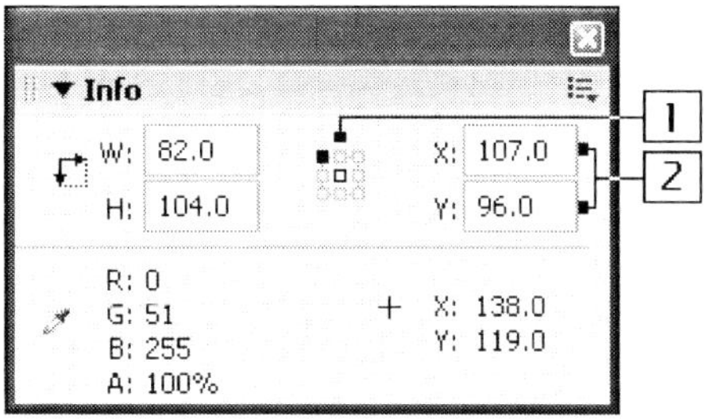

1 Click the reference point for which you are going to set the **X** and **Y** positions.

2 Give the horizontal position in the **X** field and the vertical position in the **Y** field.

C - Aligning objects

▷ Display the **Align** panel:

Window
Design Panels
Align

Ctrl **K** (PC)
⌘ **K** (Mac)

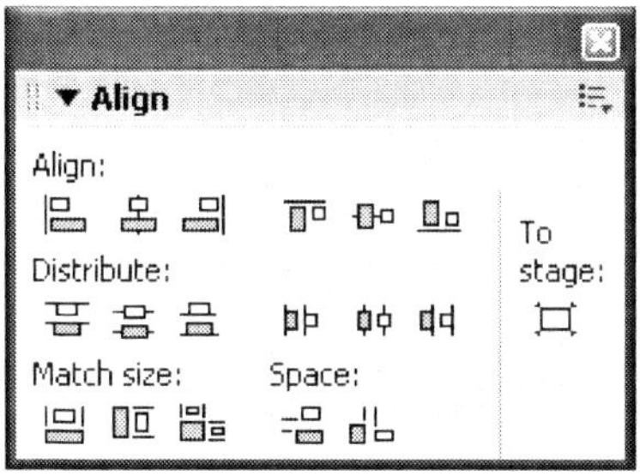

▷ Select the objects you want to align.

▷ To align the objects in relation to the stage, click the **To stage** icon .

▷ To align the objects in relation to a vertical axis, use one of these icons on the **Align** panel: 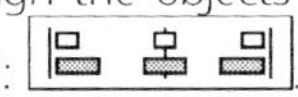.

▷ To align the objects in relation to a horizontal axis, use one of these icons on the **Align** panel: 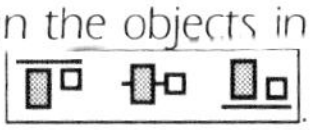.

⇨ *You can also use the **Modify - Align** menu.*

D - Distributing objects evenly

▷ Display the **Align** panel.

▷ Select the objects you want to align (there must be at least three).

▷ To distribute the objects in relation to the stage, click the **To stage** icon .

▷ To distribute the objects vertically, use one of these icons on the **Align** panel: 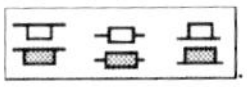.

▷ To distribute the objects horizontally, use one of these icons on the **Align** panel: 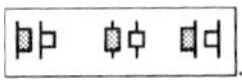.

⇨ *You can also use the **Modify - Align** menu.*

E- Changing the stacking order of objects

The objects created on the same layer are stacked in order of their creation.

▷ Select the object concerned.

▷ **Modify - Arrange**

▷ Choose one of these options or the matching shortcut:

	PC	Mac
Bring to Front	Ctrl Shift ↑	⌥ Shift ↑
Bring Forward	Ctrl ↑	⌘ ↑
Send Backward	Ctrl ↓	⌘ ↓
Send to Back	Ctrl Shift ↓	⌘ ⌥ ↓

F- Locking objects

Locked objects cannot be selected.

▷ Select the object(s).

▷ **Modify**
Arrange
Lock

Ctrl Alt **L** (PC)
⌘ ⌥ **L** (Mac)

▷ To unlock locked objects:

Modify
Arrange
Unlock All

Ctrl Alt Shift **L** (PC)
⌘ ⌥ Shift **L** (Mac)

G- Grouping objects

▷ Select the objects concerned (they must be on the same layer).

▷ **Modify**
Group

Ctrl **G** (PC)
⌘ **G** (Mac)

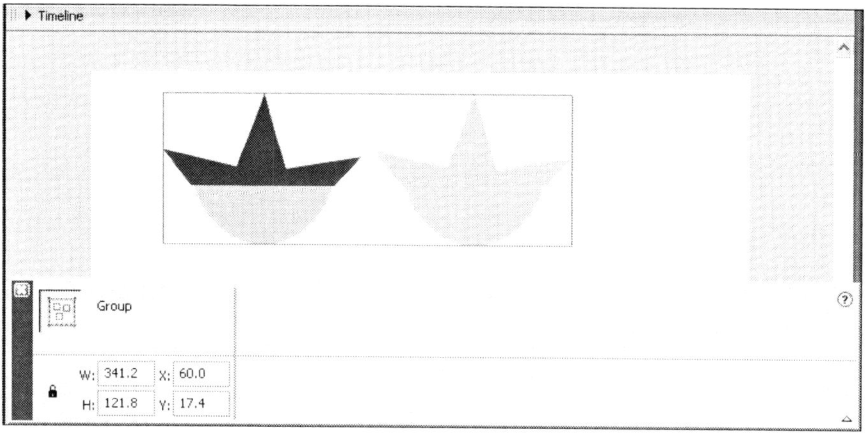

*The selection rectangle now appears around all the objects; you can now carry out actions simultaneously to all the objects in the group (moving, enlarging, reducing, etc.). The name of the object that appears in the Property inspector is **Group**.*

▷ To change the contents of the group without ungrouping the objects, use:

Edit — Double-click an item in the group
Edit Selection (PC)
Edit - Edit Selected (Mac)

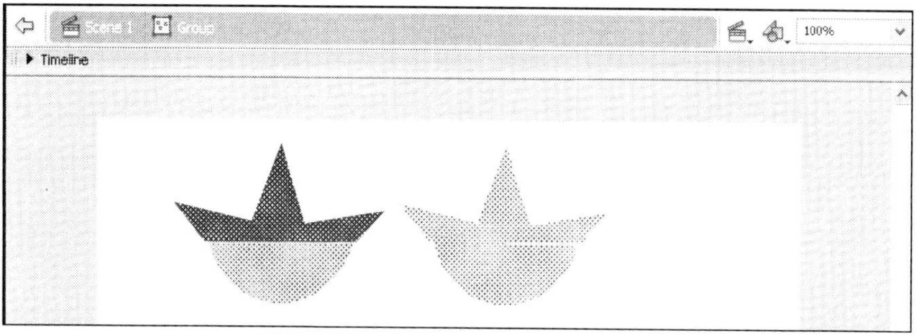

*Only the objects in the group are accessible; the word **Group** appears on the Edit bar.*

▷ Modify each object in the group as required (moving, enlarging, reducing, rotating etc...).

▷ To return to the stage:

Edit — Double-click the stage
Edit All

H - Ungrouping a group of objects

▷ Select the group.

▷ **Modify**
Ungroup

Ctrl Shift **G** (PC)
⌘ Shift **G** (Mac)

I- Breaking apart an object

This feature can break up certain types of object into distinct shapes:

- *a text block: each character becomes independent,*
- *a bitmap: this is transformed into several fills,*
- *an instance: this becomes independent from the original symbol.*

▷ Select the object(s).

▷ **Modify**
Break Apart — Ctrl **B** (PC) / ⌘ **B** (Mac)

4.3 Transforming objects

A- Modifying an object's transformation point

By default, an object's transformation point is at its centre; any transformations occur in relation to this point.

▷ Select the object.

▷ **Modify**
Transform
Free Transform

▷ A circle appears in the centre of the object: drag it to the required place.

▷ To reposition the transformation point in the object's centre, double-click it.

B- Applying a free transformation to an object

Free transformation can modify one or more objects by rotating them, resizing them or distorting them.

▷ Select the object.

▷ Click the **Free Transform** tool or press the **Q** key.

By default, the object's transformation point is at its centre; you can move this point by dragging it.

Rotating and leaning

▷ In the **Options** area of the **Tools** panel, activate the **Rotate and Skew** tool.

▷ To rotate the object, point to one of the corners of the selection rectangle and drag to turn the object around its transformation point. Hold down the Shift key to rotate the object by 45 degree angles. To rotate the object around the opposing corner of the selection rectangle and not around its transformation point, hold down the Alt (PC) or ⌥ (Mac) key.

- ▷ To lean (skew) the object over, point to one of the edges of the selection rectangle (the pointer looks like this ⇅) and drag depending on how you want to lean the object (horizontally or vertically).

Resizing

- ▷ In the **Options** area of the **Tools** panel, activate the **Scale** tool.
- ▷ To change the object's width and height, point to one of the corners of the selection rectangle and drag it. Hold down the Shift key as you drag to keep the object's proportions.
- ▷ To change only the width or the height, point to one of the side handles on the selection rectangle and drag it.

⇨ *You can also use the **Transform** panel (cf. heading below) or the **Modify - Transform - Scale** command.*

Distorting

You can only this transformation to shapes. To distort a bitmap or text, you first need to convert the picture or characters into shape objects.

- ▷ In the **Options** area of the **Tools** panel, activate the **Distort** tool.
- ▷ Point to one of the handles on the selection rectangle and drag to achieve the required effect.

⇨ *You can also use the **Modify - Transform - Distort** command.*

C - Using the Transform panel

▷ **Window**
Design Panels
Transform

Ctrl **T** (PC)
⌘ **T** (Mac)

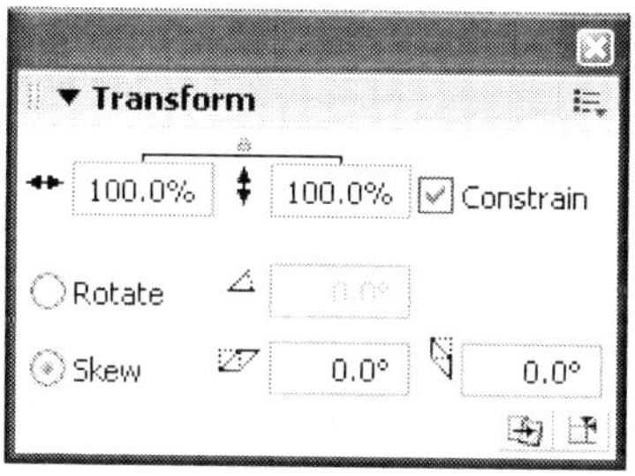

- ▷ To resize the object, indicate the width and height in the 100.0% and 100.0% fields. Tick the **Constrain** check box to keep the proportions between width and height.

⇨ *You can also modify the width and height in the **Info** panel.*

- ▷ To rotate the selected object, give a rotation angle in the appropriate box.

⇨ *Another way of rotating an object by 90 degrees (clockwise or counter-clockwise) is to use **Modify - Transform - Rotate 90° CW** or **Rotate 90° CCW**.*

- To lean over the object, activate the **Skew** option and specify how far it should lean in the **Skew horizontally** [-15.0°] and/or **Skew vertically** box [165.0°].
- To make a copy of the object and transform the copy, click the **Copy and transform** button.
- To cancel the transformation you just made to the object, click the **Reset** button (as long as the object has not been deselected).

⇨ *Another way of resizing and rotating an object is to use* ***Modify - Transform - Scale and Rotate*** *(Ctrl Alt* ***S*** *(PC) or* ⌘ ⌥ ***S*** *(Mac).*

D-Applying the same dimensions to different objects

- Select the objects.
- Click one of these buttons on the **Align** panel to **Match width, Match height** or **Match width and height**.

E-Flipping an object

- Select the object or group of objects.
- **Modify - Transform**
  Flip Vertical or **Flip Horizontal**

F-Cancelling transformations

To apply this to a single object, it must not have been deselected since the transformation (this is not the case for a group of objects).

- If applicable, select the group of objects.
- **Modify**
  Transform
  Remove Transform

  Ctrl ⇧Shift **Z** (PC)
  ⌘ ⇧Shift **Z** (Mac)

  or
  Click the **Reset** button on the **Transform** panel.

5.1 Principles of animation

A - Flash animation overview

In Flash, you can create three different types of animation:

- frame-by-frame animation:

The contents of the stage differ with each frame in the Timeline ; as the movie plays, the series of frames produces an animation effect.

- shape tweening:

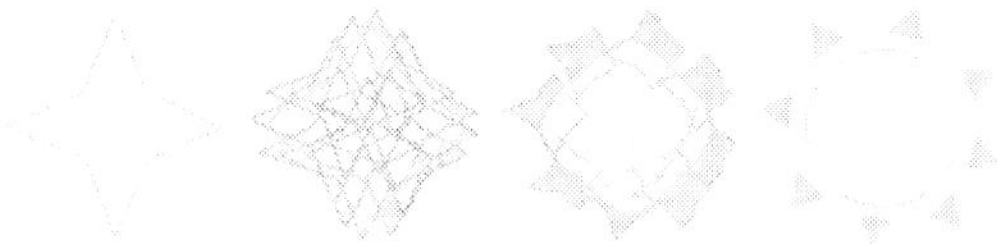

An object is placed on the stage at the starting frame, and another is placed at the ending frame. Once you apply shape tweening, Flash generates intermediate frames that transform the object.

- motion tweening:

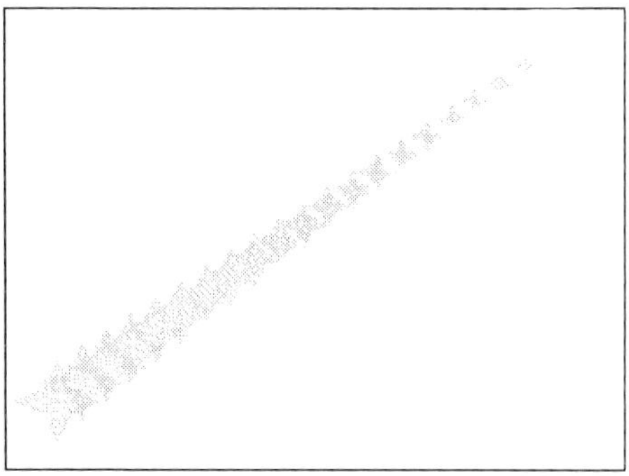

An object is placed on the stage at the starting frame, and then placed in another position at the ending frame. Once you apply motion tweening, Flash generates intermediate frames that move the object. You can define the path along which the movement will occur.

⇨ *A Flash movie can be cut into mini-movies called sequences (cf. 6.3 - Movie structure).*

B- Playing a movie

▷ Display the **Controller** bar:

Window - Toolbars - Controller

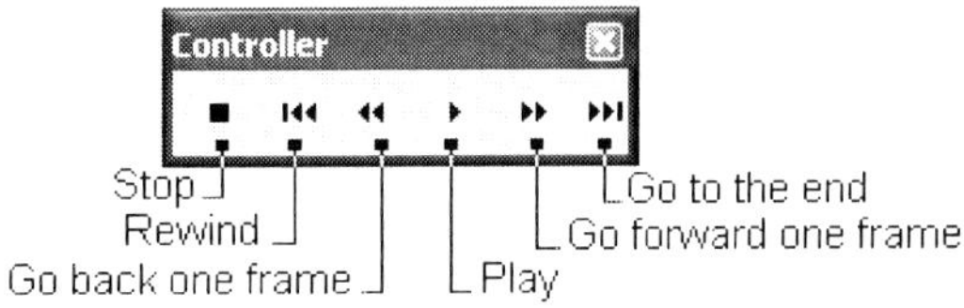

*You can also use the options in the **Control** menu.*

▷ To set up how the movie should play, use these options from the **Control** menu: **Loop Playback**, **Play All Scenes**, **Mute Sounds** (to play the movie without any of its sounds).

C- Using Onion skin mode

When you create an animation, you cannot see all the frame contents (what comes before and after) on one or more layers at the same time on the stage. When you activate Onion skin mode, objects in frames that come before or after the active frame appear (albeit in a dimmed form) so you can get a global view of the animation.

▷ In the **Timeline**, click the **Onion Skin** button 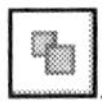.

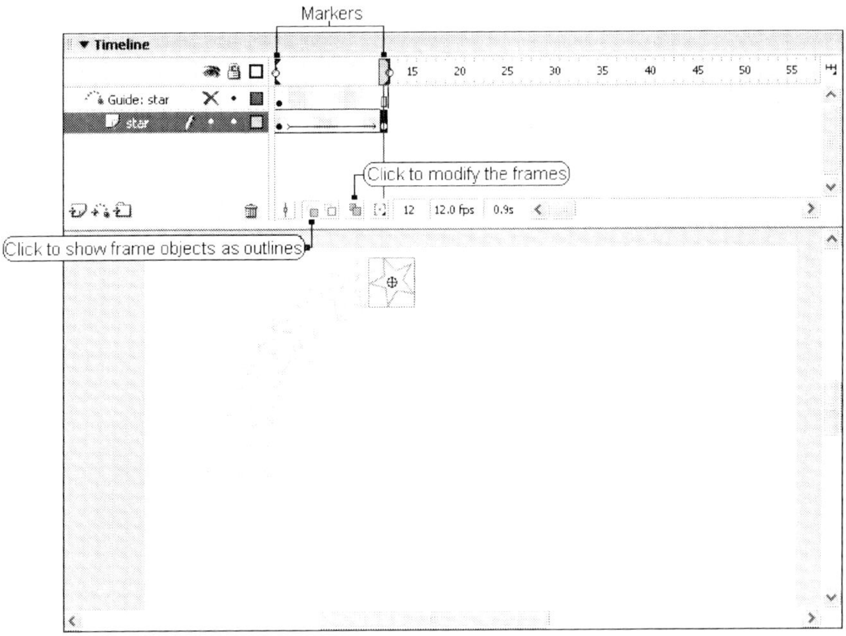

▷ To set the range of frames you want to view, drag the Onion skin markers, or choose one of these options by clicking the **Modify Onion Markers** button.

Always Show Markers	Shows the onion skin markers even if you are not in Onion skin mode.
Anchor Onion	Locks the onion skin markers.
Onion 2	Spreads the markers over the two frames to the right and left of the active frame.
Onion 5	Spreads the markers over the five frames to the right and left of the active frame.
Onion All	Spreads the markers over all the frames on either side of the current frame.

5.2 Frame-by-frame animation

A-Creating a frame-by-frame animation

Here is an example:

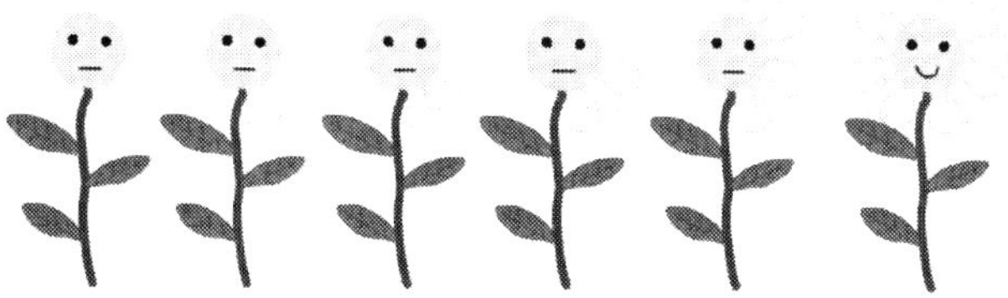

▷ Click the name of the layer on which you want to insert the objects.

▷ Click the frame where the animation should start and if necessary, insert a keyframe:

Insert
Timeline
Keyframe F6

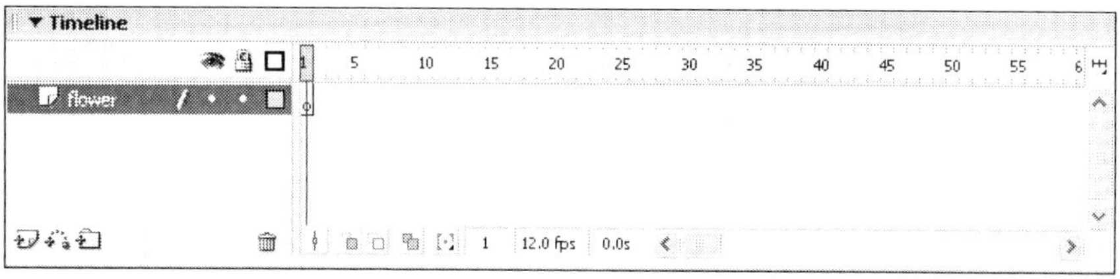

A keyframe appears in the Timeline: it contains a white circle.

▷ Create or insert the object on the stage.

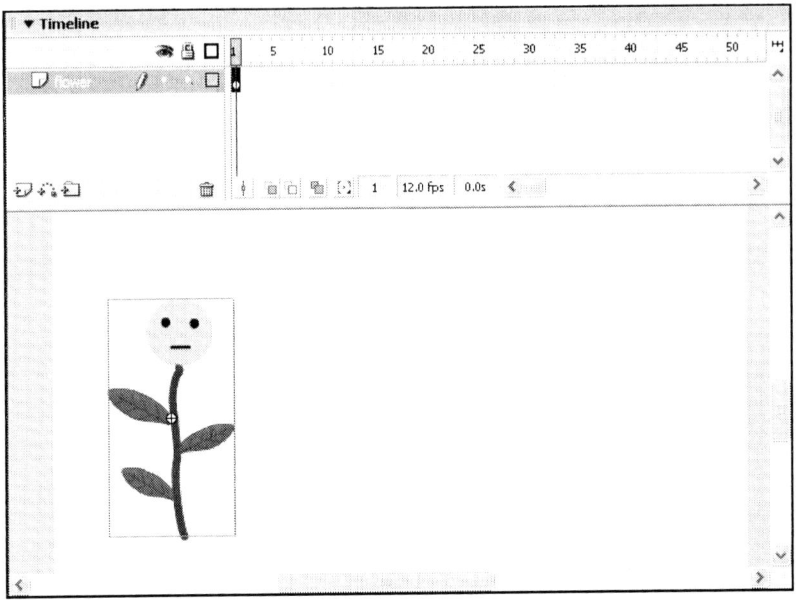

The keyframe is no longer blank: the white circle turns black (but if the frame is selected in the Timeline, as it is here, it will appear in inverse video, with a black frame and a white circle).

▷ Click the next frame and insert another keyframe.

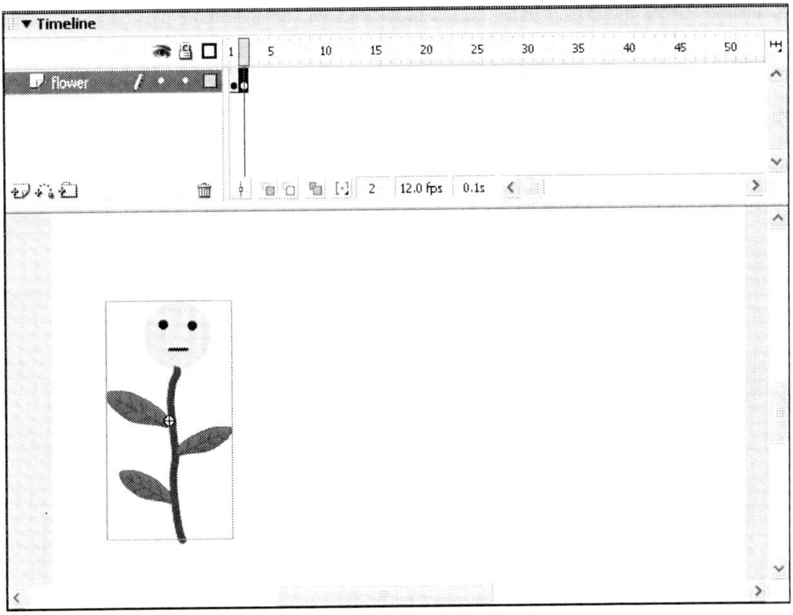

A new keyframe appears: it contains the same object as the first frame (you can check here that the first frame contains a black dot).

▷ Edit the object on the stage.

The first petal is added to the flower.

▷ Repeat these last two steps to define each frame of the animation.

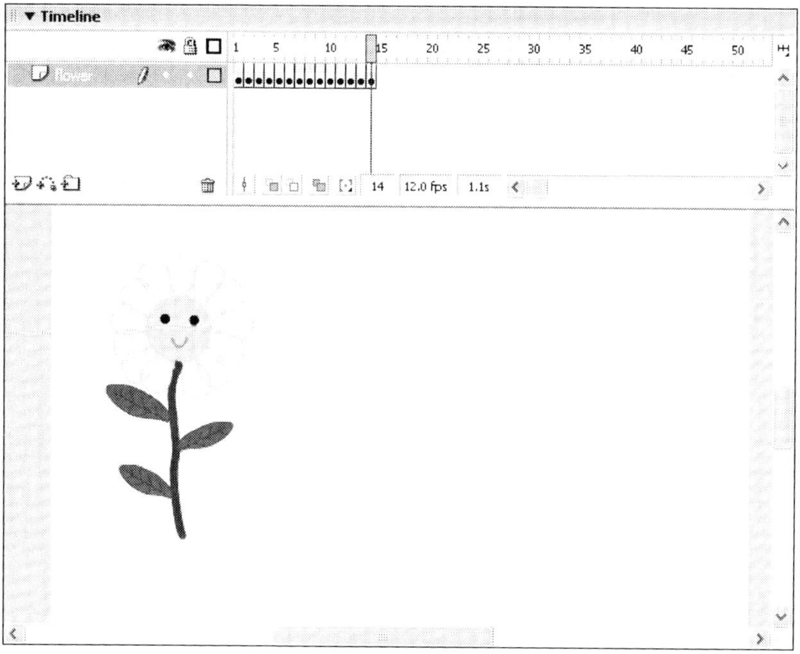

Here, there are 14 frames in this animation.

▷ Play the movie to view the animation:

Control
Play ▶ Enter

⇨ *This type of animation makes for a larger file size compared to tweening.*

5.3 Tweening

A-Creating a motion tween

Without a guide layer

▷ If necessary, insert the first keyframe.

▷ Display the Property inspector.

▷ Create the first frame of the tween by placing an object or symbol on the stage.

▷ If you drew the object yourself, you need to convert it into a symbol: **Modify** - **Convert to Symbol** or F8 then click **OK**.

Using symbols is described in a later chapter.

▷ Click the last frame in the tween and use **Insert - Timeline - Keyframe**.

▷ Make your changes to the layer's contents: move the object, resize it, rotate or skew it, etc.

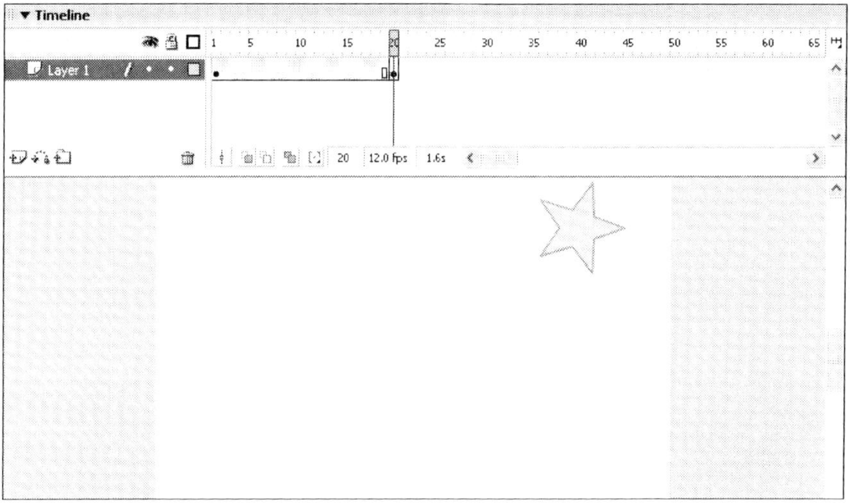

▷ Click one of the frames in the tween, go into the Property inspector, open the **Tween** pop-up menu and choose the **Motion** option.

The motion tween is represented in the Timeline by an arrow on a blue background.

If you activate Onion skin mode, you can see the different frames in the animation:

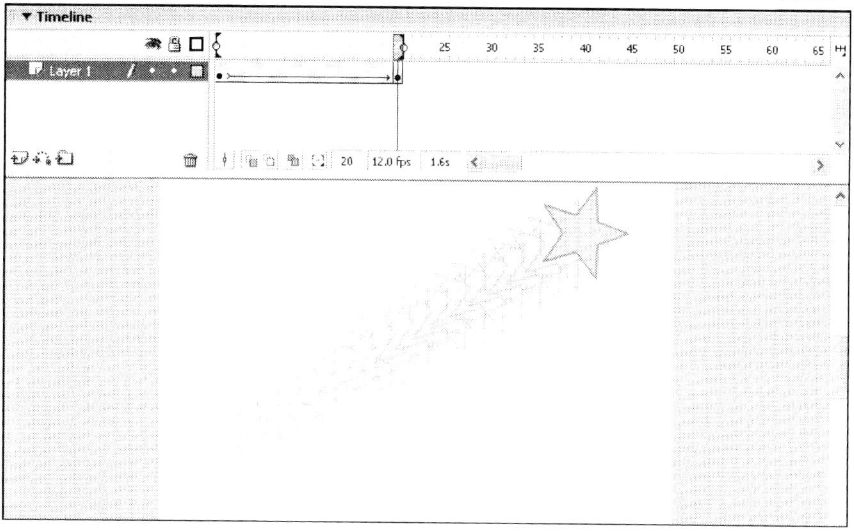

By default, the path that the tween runs along is a straight line.

⇨ *You can also display a frame's shortcut menu and choose* ***Create Motion Tween*** *or use the* ***Insert - Timeline - Create Motion Tween*** *command.*

Using a guide layer

The guide layer contains a path that your object can follow during tweening.

▷ Create a motion tween (cf. previous subheading).

▷ Select the layer on which the motion tween was created.

▷ **Insert**
Timeline
Motion Guide

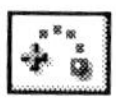 (**Timeline**)

A guide layer appears above the selected layer.

▷ Draw the path in the guide layer.

▷ Click the first frame of the tween then position the object's transformation point on the point that marks the start of the path.

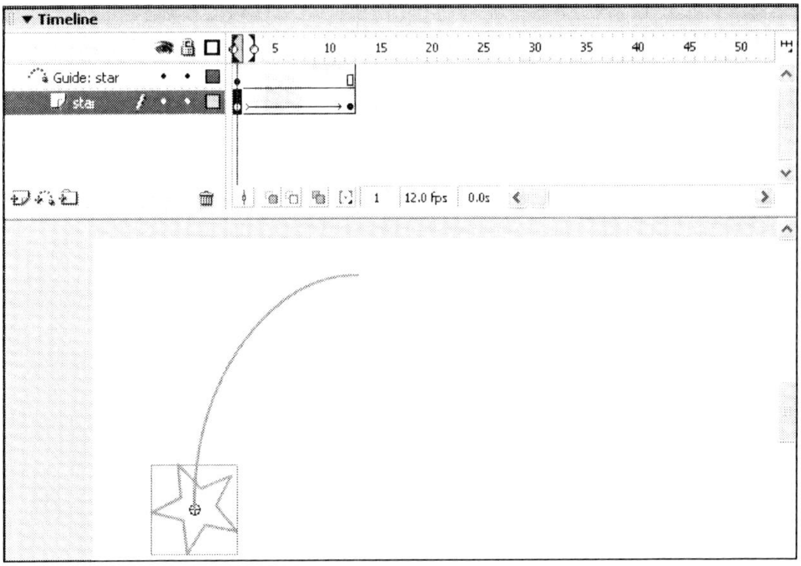

▷ Click the last frame of the tween and position the object's transformation point on the point that marks the end of the path.

▷ Click one of the frames in the tween, go into the Property inspector, and tick the **Orient to path** option to orient the baseline of the object towards the path as it moves. Tick the **Snap** option to snap the object to its motion guide by its alignment point.

▷ Start playing the movie.

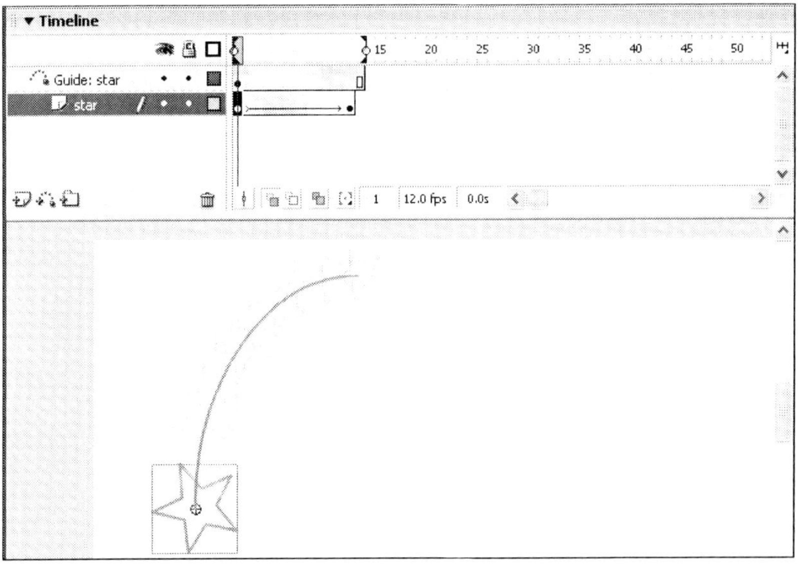

Here, Onion skin mode has been turned on so you can see all the frames along the motion path.

⇨ *You can hide the guide layer if you do not want to show the guide path, making the animation easier to see.*

⇨ *To link a layer containing a motion tween to a guide layer, place this layer under the guide layer; conversely, to break the link between a motion tween layer and its guide layer, place it above the guide layer or use the* ***Modify - Timeline - Layer Properties*** *command and choose* ***Normal*** *as the layer* ***Type****.*

B - Modifying a motion tween's properties

▷ Click one of the frames in the motion tween.

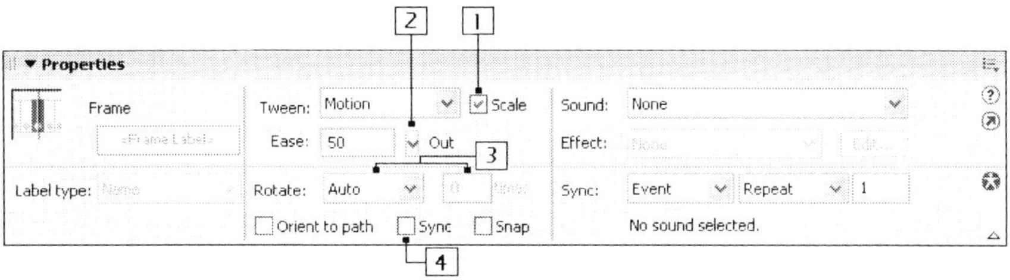

1 If your tween changes the size of the object, tick this option so that the change happens gradually.

2 If you want your motion tween to accelerate as it goes on, choose a value between 0 and 100. Conversely, if you want the movement to slow down progressively, choose a value between -1 and -100.

3 To rotate the object during tweening, choose **CW** (clockwise) or **CCW** (counter-clockwise) and specify how many times it must rotate; if you choose **Auto**, the rotation happens over the length of the tween.

4 Tick this option to match the number of frames in the tween with the number of frames in the Timeline.

C - Creating a shape tween

Shape tweening works on the same principle as image morphing: it transforms one shape into another (for example, a star into a sun).

▷ If necessary, insert the first keyframe.

▷ Draw or insert the shape on the stage.

This shape must have stroke and fill. If it is a symbol, a bitmap or a text, you need to break it apart.

▷ Insert a keyframe where the tween should end.

▷ Define the last keyframe by modifying the shape or by deleting it and creating a different one.

▷ Click one of the frames in the tween.

▷ In the Property inspector choose the **Shape** option in the **Tween** pop-up menu.

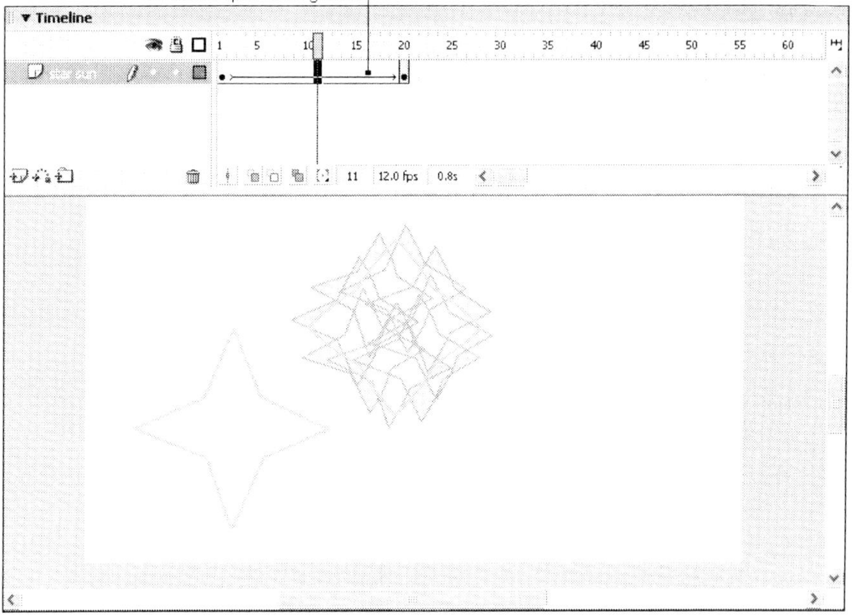

D-Using shape hints

Shape hints help to define more complex shape changes during tweening, by providing points from which the tween can be calculated.

▷ Select the first keyframe for the shape tween.

▷ **Modify**
Shape
Add Shape Hint

Ctrl ⇧Shift **H** (PC)
⌘ ⇧Shift **H** (Mac)

The shape hint appears as a small red circle containing the letter "a".

▷ Move it to the place on the shape where you want to mark the starting point.

▷ Select the last keyframe of the tween.

It appears with the same shape hint.

▷ Move the shape hint to the place where the ending point should be.

▷ If necessary, insert other shape hints using the same procedure.

▷ To display all the shape hints, click a keyframe and use:

View
Show Shape Hints

Ctrl Alt **H** (PC)
⌘ ⌥ **H** (Mac)

▷ To remove a shape hint, drag it off the stage.

▷ To remove all the shape hints, click a keyframe and activate the **Remove All Hints** in the **Modify - Shape** menu.

⇨ *Shape hints can only be seen when the playhead is on a keyframe.*

E - Modifying a shape tween's properties

▷ Click one of the tween's frames.

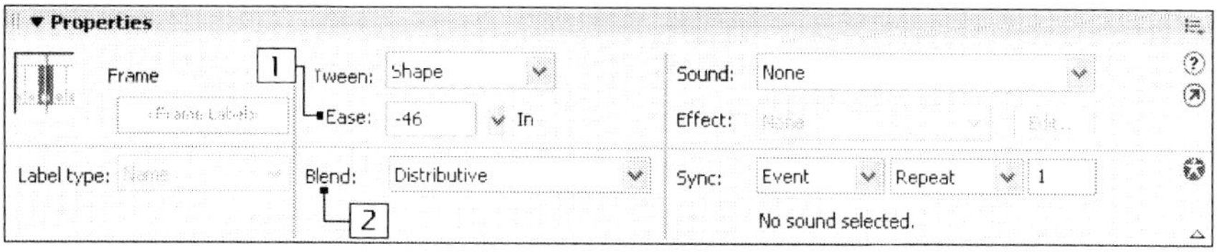

[1] If you want your tween to accelerate as it goes on, choose a value between 0 and 100. If you want the movement to slow down progressively, choose a value between -1 and -100.

[2] Choose **Distributive** if you want to smooth the intermediate forms or **Angular** to preserve corners.

5.4 Masks

A - Creating a mask layer

A mask layer can hide a certain part of a layer. As the movie plays, the mask put in motion creates a transition effect, hiding or displaying the layer's contents:

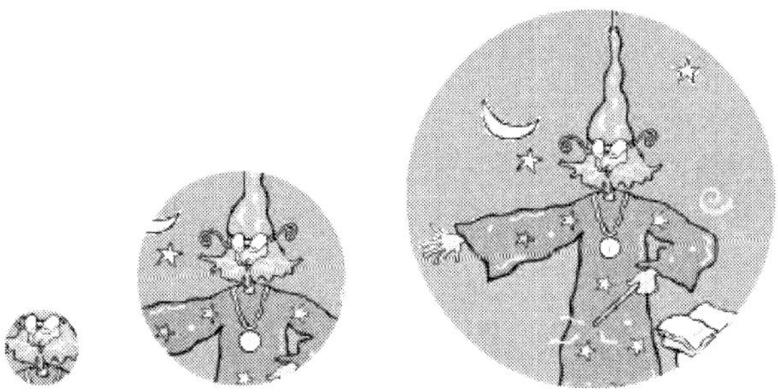

▷ Select or create the background layer(s): the mask will lie on top of this to hide it.

▷ Create a new layer, which will be the mask layer.

▷ Select the frame where the masking effect will begin then draw or insert the "hole" shape that is the transparent area of the mask.

Even if this shape contains fill, it will appear transparent as the movie plays.

▷ Stretch the keyframe span on the mask layer so it is the same length as the other layers (cf. 5.5 - D - Inserting one or more frames).

▷ Apply a shape or motion tween to the shape on the mask layer.

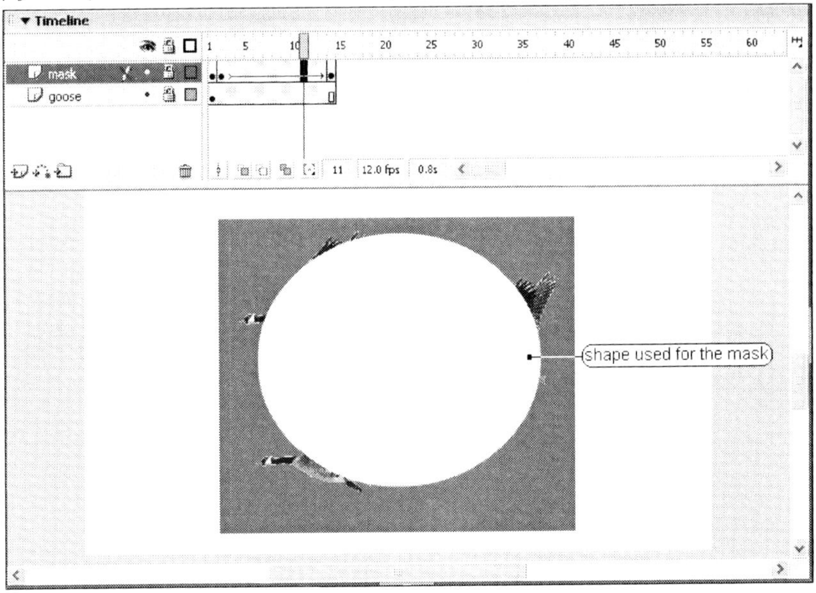

▷ Right-click (PC) or Ctrl-click (Mac) the layer and take the **Mask** option.

The layer becomes a mask layer; it is symbolised by an icon in the ***Timeline****.*

▷ Lock the layers.

The mask effect can now be seen.

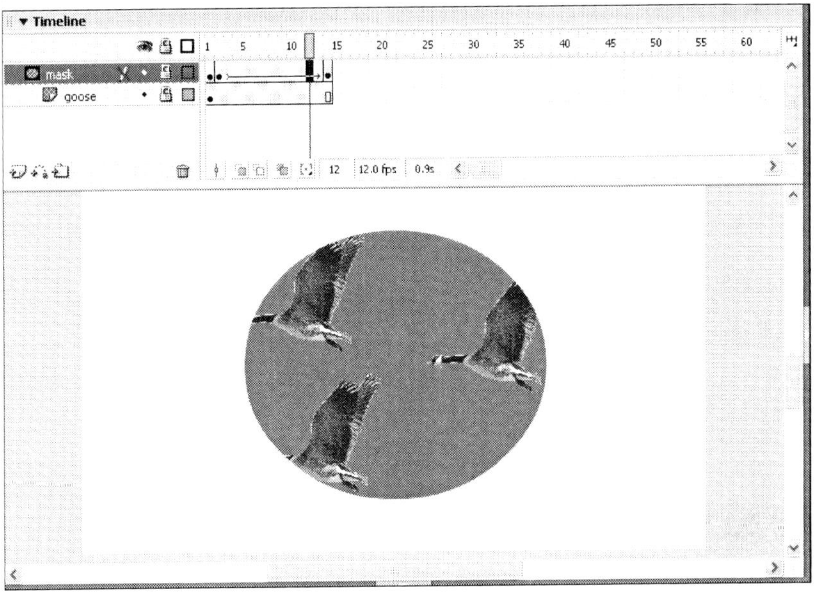

▷ Start playing the movie.

B - Managing a mask layer

▷ To edit a mask layer or the layer masked by it, you must unlock the layers.

▷ To associate an existing layer with a mask layer, drag that layer under the mask layer.

▷ To separate a layer from a mask layer, display its properties (**Modify - Timeline - Layer Properties**) and activate the **Normal** option.

5.5 Managing frames in the Timeline

A - Changing how the Timeline displays frames

▷ Click the button and activate the options that you require.

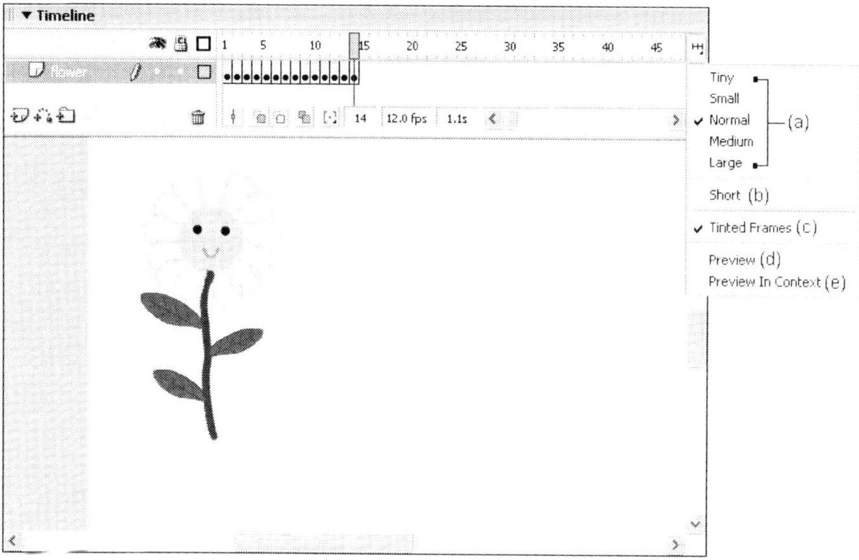

(a) Define the size of the frames.

(b) Reduces the height of the frames.

(c) Colours the frame backgrounds according to the tweening applied.

(d) The contents of each keyframe appear in a thumbnail.

(e) The entire stage appears in miniature on each thumbnail.

⇨ *A movie can contain a large number of frames that cannot all be visible in the **Timeline** window. The **Center frame** button rapidly scrolls through the Timeline window's contents to display the frame in which the playhead is located.*

B- Different types of frame

There are two types of frame:

- the standard frame represented by ; a series of frames is called a sequence, with a starting frame represented by and the end or static frame by .
- the keyframe is used to mark a change in the movie: it is represented by this symbol or by this one if it is placed at a point where the stage is empty.

C- Selecting frames

▷ To select a frame, click it.

▷ To select several adjacent frames, click the first frame, press the [Shift] key and click the last frame. You can also hold down the [Ctrl] (PC) or [⌘] (Mac) key and drag.

▷ To select all the frames between two keyframes, double-click one of the intermediate frames.

▷ To select a shape or motion tween, click one of the frames in it.

▷ To select all the frames on a layer, click that layer.

D- Inserting one or more frames

Creating a sequence

▷ If necessary, insert a first keyframe using **Insert - Timeline - Keyframe**.

▷ Place the playhead on the last frame of the sequence you want to create, then:

- insert an end frame using **Insert - Timeline - Frame** or [F5]:

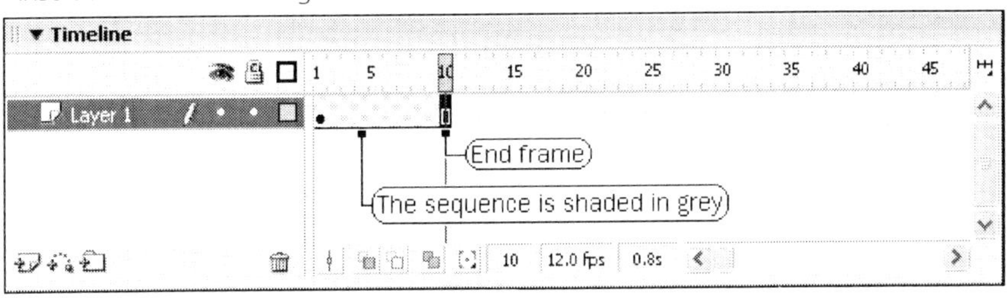

- Insert a keyframe with **Insert - Timeline - Keyframe** or F6:

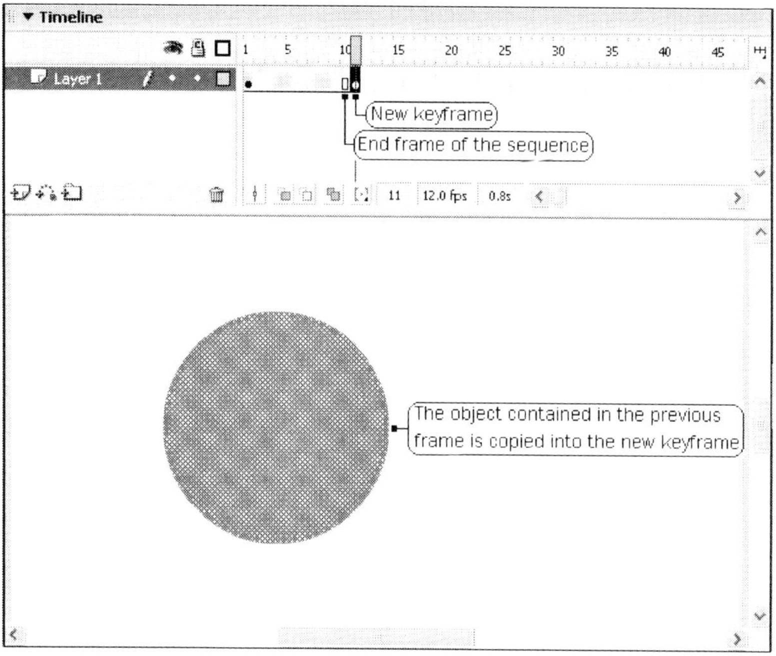

- insert an empty keyframe using **Insert - Timeline - Blank Keyframe** or F7:

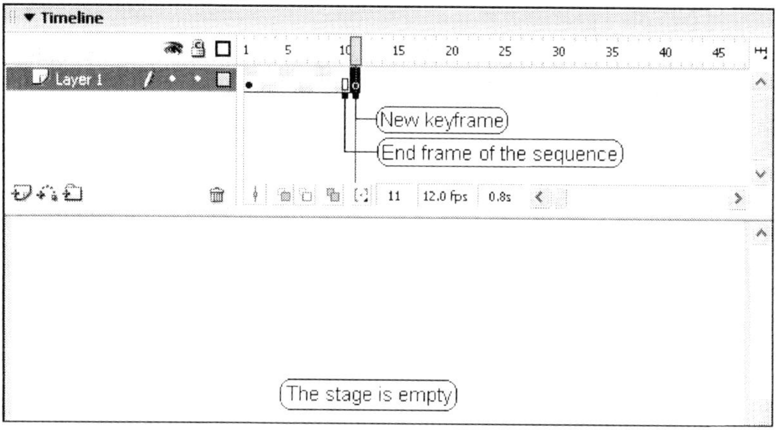

⇨ *You can convert one (or more) frames using the **Modify - Timeline - Convert to Keyframes** or **Convert to Blank Keyframes** command.*

⇨ *If you want to convert a keyframe to a frame, select the keyframe and use **Modify - Timeline - Clear Keyframe** or* Shift F6.

Changing the range of a sequence

▷ To extend the length of a sequence, drag the end frame to the right if the frames to the right of it are blank; you can also click one of the frames to the right and use the **Frame, Keyframe** or **Blank Keyframe** options in the **Insert - Timeline** menu.

If there is another sequence to the right of the one you wish to extend, go to the sequence you are extending and select as many frames as you want to add of new ones.

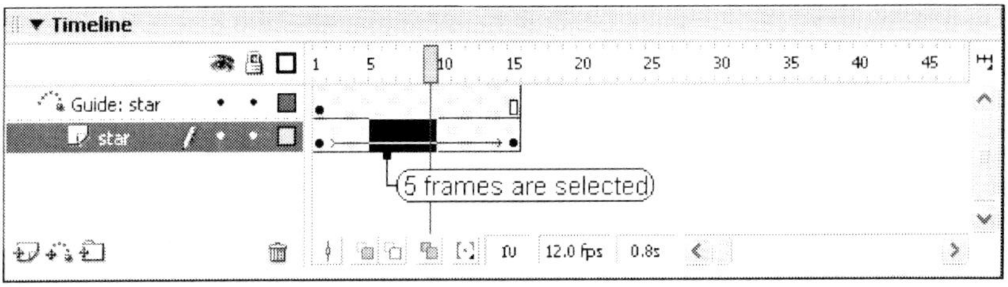

▷ **Insert** [F5]
Timeline
Frame

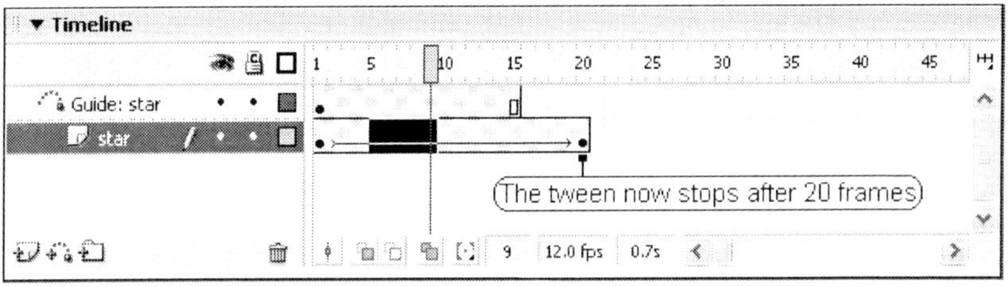

On this example, you would then need to extend the sequence for the guide layer.

▷ To shorten a sequence, select the frames you want to remove and use **Edit - Timeline - Remove Frames** or [Shift] [F5].

E - Deleting frames

▷ Select the frame(s) that you want to delete.

▷ **Edit** [Shift] [F5]
Timeline
Remove Frames

You can also open the shortcut menu and click the ***Remove Frames*** *option.*

F - Clearing a keyframe

▷ Select the keyframe you wish to clear.

▷ **Modify** [Shift] [F6]
Timeline
Clear Keyframe

*You can also open the shortcut menu and click the **Clear Keyframe** option.*

⇨ *The Del (PC) or ⌘ ← (Mac) key transforms a keyframe into a blank keyframe.*

G-Copying or moving frames

▷ To move a sequence, select the frames then drag them to the required place. Hold down Alt (PC) or ⌥ (Mac) if you want to copy the selection.

▷ To copy the selected frames, use:

Edit — Ctrl Alt **C** (PC)
Timeline — ⌘ ⌥ **C** (Mac)
Copy Frames

To cut the selected frames, use:

Edit — Ctrl Alt **X** (PC)
Timeline — ⌘ ⌥ **X** (Mac)
Cut Frames

▷ Click the frame where you want to paste the cut/copied range.

Edit — Ctrl Alt **V** (PC)
Timeline — ⌘ ⌥ **V** (Mac)
Paste Frames

H-Moving an entire animation

With this technique you can move an entire animation sequence (layer content and frames) onto the stage in one action.

▷ Check that the layers concerned are not locked.

▷ Click the **Edit Multiple Frames** button.

▷ Modify the span of the Onion skin markers to define which frames are involved.

▷ Select these frames using **Edit - Select All**.

▷ Drag the selection onto the stage.

I- Swapping frames in a sequence

▷ Select the frames concerned (there must be at least one keyframe at the beginning and at the end of the sequence).

Modify - Timeline - Reverse Frames

6.1 Managing symbols

Most of the items created or imported into Flash can be managed as symbols. Symbols are stored in the library. When you place them on the stage, you create an instance of the symbol. If you edit the original symbol, the instances of that symbol are updated automatically.

Using symbols makes for movies with a smaller file size, as the file size does not increase, no matter how many instances you create. Some actions can only be carried out with symbols.

A - Creating a symbol

To create a symbol, you can convert an object, draw the symbol or import the required item.

Converting an object into a symbol

▷ Select the object on the stage.

▷ **Modify - Convert to Symbol** or F8

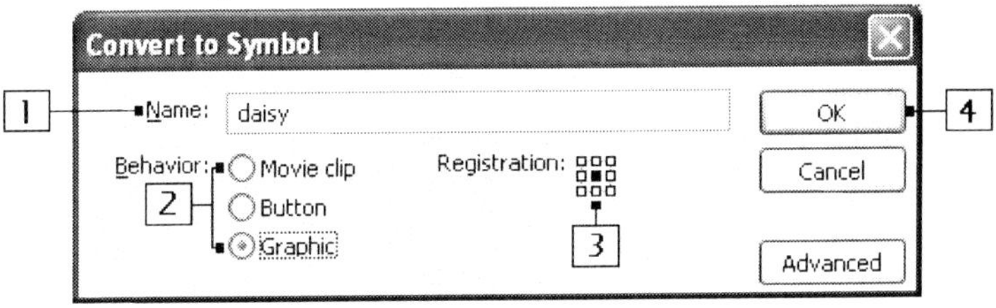

1 Give a name for the symbol.

2 Indicate the type of symbol.

Movie clip	If the symbol is a movie clip.
Button	If the symbol is an action button.
Graphic	If the symbol is a shape or drawing object. You cannot apply interactivity or sound to a graphic symbol.

3 Define the transformation point.

4 Create the symbol.

The symbol then appears in the Library.

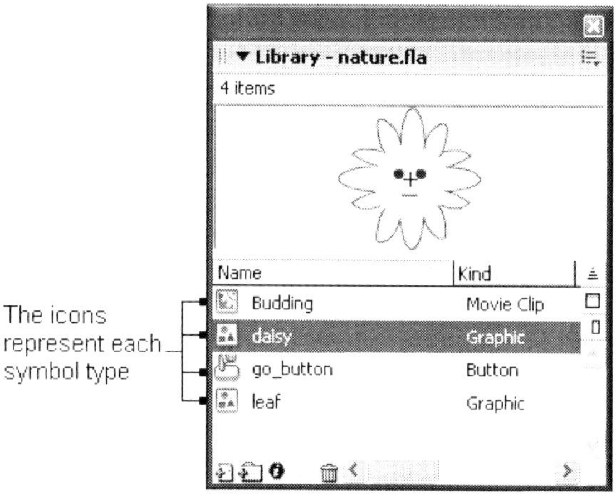

Creating a new symbol

▷ **Insert**
New Symbol Ctrl F8 (PC) ⌘ F8 (Mac)

You can also click the button on the ***Library*** *panel or choose the* ***New Symbol*** *command in its* ***Options*** *menu* .

▷ Give a **Name** for the symbol, its type and its transformation point.

▷ Confirm with **OK**.

This takes you into symbol editing mode.

▷ Make your symbol, using the various drawing tools or by importing items.

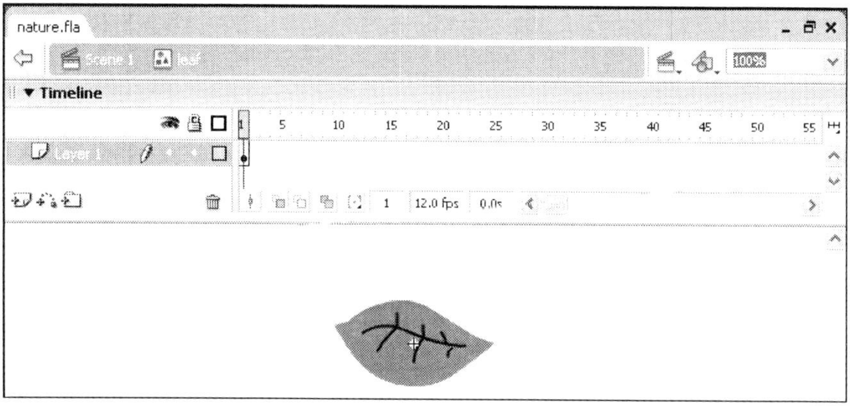

▷ To leave symbol editing mode, click the name of the scene in the **Edit** bar, or use **Edit - Edit Document** (Ctrl **E** (PC) or ⌘ **E** (Mac)) or choose a scene from the list on the **Edit Scene** button on the **Edit** bar.

OPTIMISATION

B - Creating an instance of a symbol

▷ Put the symbol concerned on the stage by dragging it from the **Library** panel.

▷ If the symbol is a Button or Movie clip type, you can name the symbol instance in the Property inspector.

C - Editing a symbol

All the instances of that symbol will be subsequently updated.

Editing a symbol directly on the stage

▷ Select the symbol instance on the stage.

▷ **Edit** double-click the instance
Edit in Place

The colours fade on the other objects on the stage.

▷ Make your changes to the symbol.

▷ Confirm by clicking the name of the **Scene** in the **Edit** bar or with **Edit - Edit Document** (Ctrl **E** (PC) or ⌘ **E** (Mac)) or by choosing a scene from the list on the **Edit Scene** button on the **Edit** bar.

Editing a symbol in a new window

You can edit the symbol without the other stage items being present.

▷ Right-click (PC) or Ctrl-click (Mac) the instance and choose **Edit in New Window**.

▷ Make your changes to the symbol.

▷ To see the result on the stage, click the window tab for the main timeline.

▷ Confirm with **Edit - Edit Document** (Ctrl **E** (PC) or ⌘ **E** (Mac)) or by choosing a scene from the list on the **Edit Scene** button on the **Edit** bar.

Editing a symbol in symbol editing mode

With this method, only the symbol's timeline is displayed.

▷ Select the symbol instance on the stage.

Edit Double-click the symbol Ctrl **E** (PC)
Edit Symbols in the Library ⌘ **E** (Mac)

▷ Make your changes to the symbol.

▷ Confirm with **Edit - Edit Document** (Ctrl **E** (PC) or ⌘ **E** (Mac)) or by choosing a scene from the list on the **Edit Scene** button on the **Edit** bar.

⇨ *To delete a symbol, select it in the Library and click* 🗑.

D-Changing an instance's colour

This change affects only the instance, not the original symbol. It can be applied to any of the three types of symbol.

▷ Select the symbol instance on the stage.

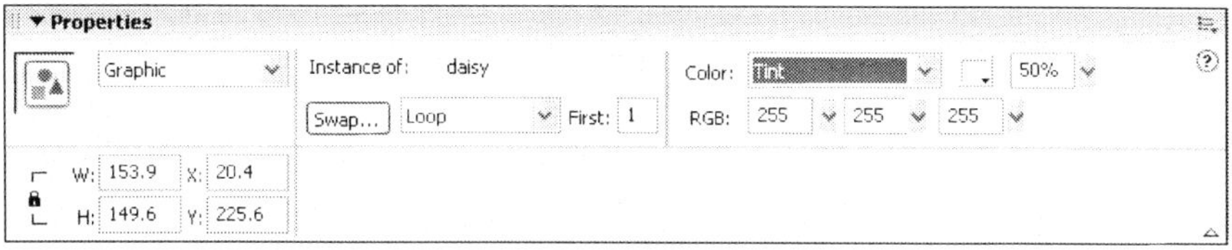

▷ Open the **Color** pop-up menu on the Property inspector and choose the effect you wish to apply:

Brightness To change the light intensity.

Tint To apply another colour:

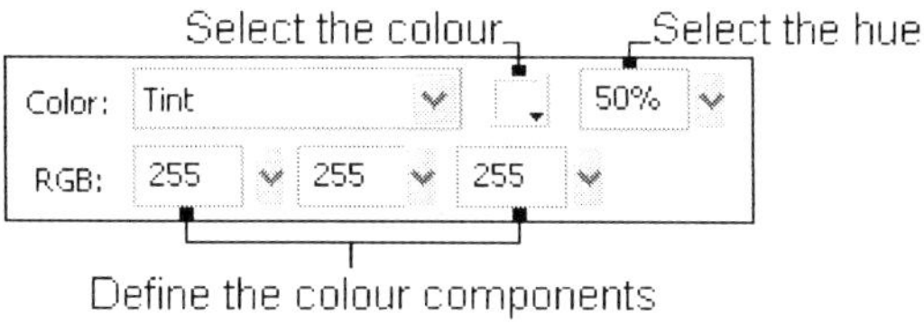

Alpha To apply a level of transparency between 0% (transparent) and 100% (opaque). This property can be used to make a symbol appear or disappear progressively.

Advanced Click the **Settings** button to define the RGB values and the transparency level as percentages:

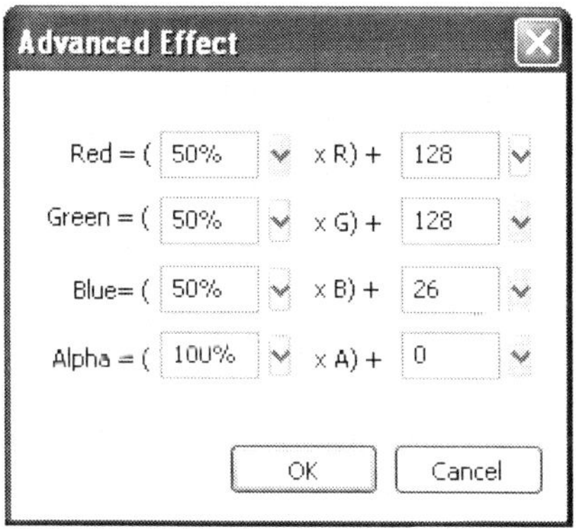

⇨ *You can resize or rotate an instance without affecting the other instances.*

⇨ *Apart from these changes you can modify a symbol instance without affect the original symbol by breaking it apart and transforming it into a shape (**Modify - Break Apart**).*

E- Swapping symbols

▷ Select the instance concerned.

▷ Click the **Swap** button on the Property inspector.

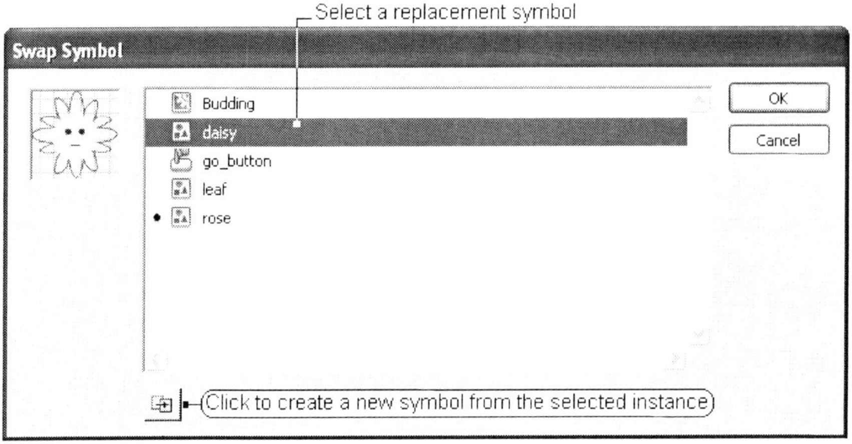

F- Creating an interactive button

▷ **Insert**
New Symbol — Ctrl F8 (PC) / ⌘ F8 (Mac)

▷ Give a **Name** for the symbol, and activate **Button** as the type.

▷ Confirm with **OK** to go into symbol editing mode.

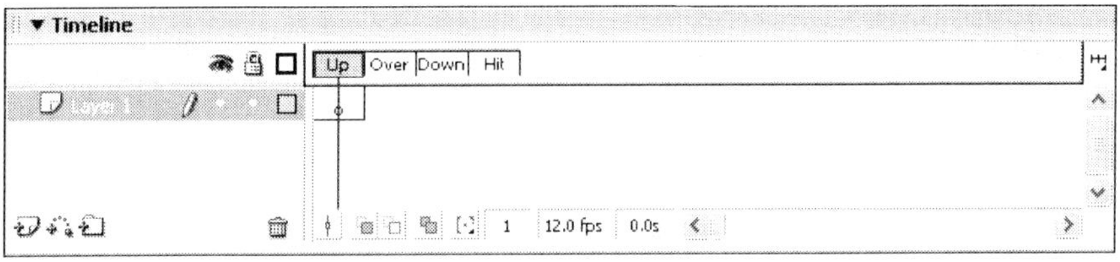

The first frame that appears in the Timeline is a blank keyframe. The time-based line is replaced by four frames, each corresponding to a different button state.

- ▷ Select the first frame (**Up**) then create or import an object onto the stage that will correspond to the button as it appears on the stage.

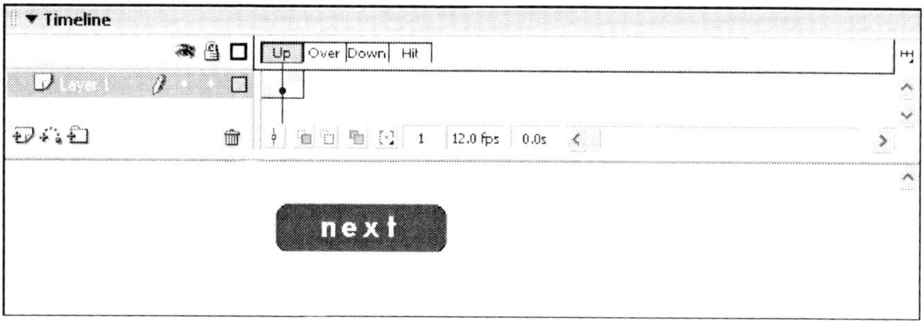

- ▷ Click the **Over** frame and insert a keyframe (**Insert - Timeline - Keyframe**).

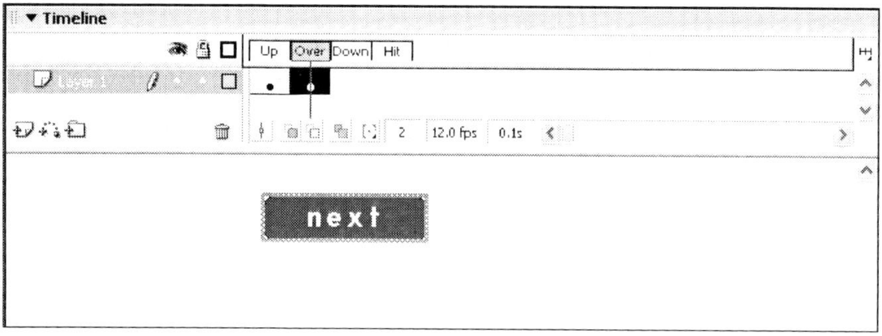

*The drawing object that belonged to the **Up** frame is carried over to the **Over** frame.*

- ▷ Modify the object for the **Over** frame in order to distinguish the different states of the button. This state is the button as it appears when the pointer is moved onto it.
- ▷ Use the same technique to create the **Down** frame: this shows the button as it appears when the user clicks it.
- ▷ Next, create the **Hit** frame: this defines the area in which the user can click.

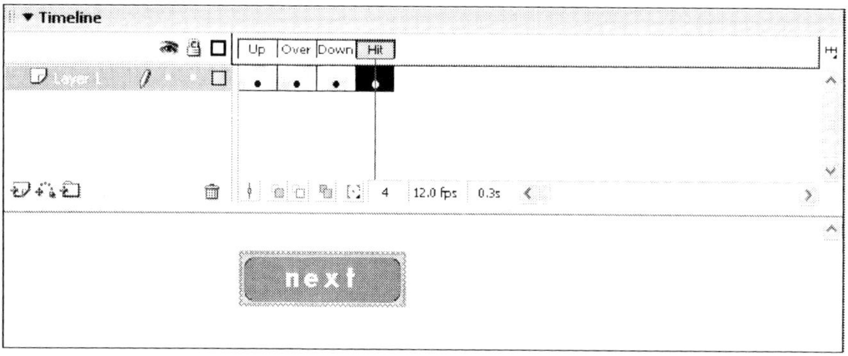

The "clickable" area may be larger or smaller than the actual button.

- ▷ Return to the stage (**Edit - Edit Document**).
- ▷ To insert the button on the stage, drag its symbol from the Library onto the stage.

⇨ *To test whether a button works, activate the* ***Enable Simple Buttons*** *command in the* ***Control*** *menu and click the button to see the effect produced (you can also select the symbol and click the* ▶ *play button on the* ***Library*** *panel).*

Setting a button's properties

▷ Select an instance of the button.

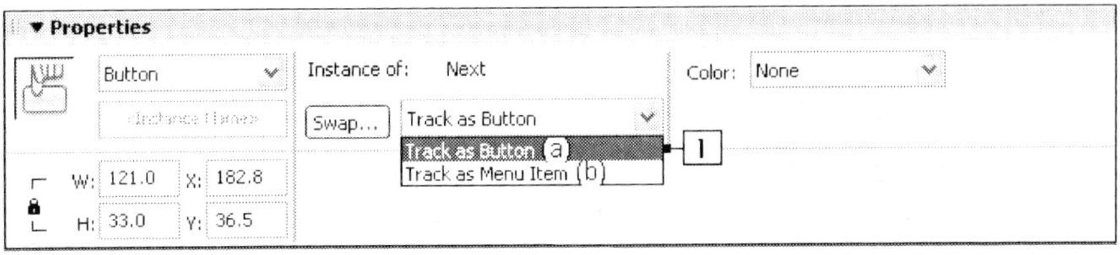

1 Choose one of these options:

(a) so the button does not react when the pointer moves over it with the mouse button pressed down.

(b) so the button uses the **Down** state when the pointer moves over it if the mouse button is already pressed down. This option is used to highlight an option pointed to in a menu (when you point to the option, the option background or its text may for example change colour).

G-Creating a font symbol

Creating a font symbol imports a font into the Library so it can be used in any movie, without having to embed it in the movie.

▷ Display the Library that will contain the font symbol:

Window - Library or F11 (PC) or ⌘ **L** (Mac)

▷ Open the Library's **Options** menu and choose **New Font**.

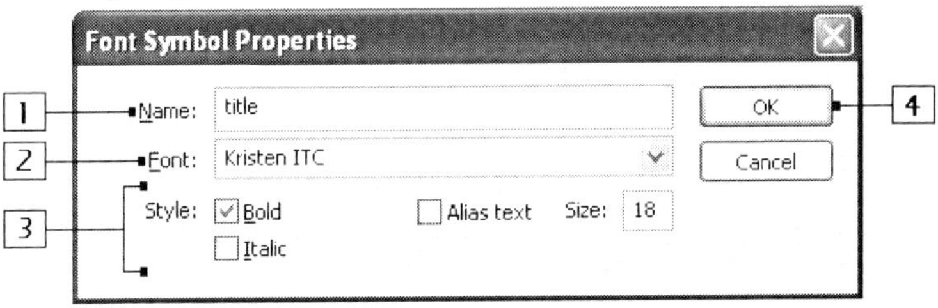

1 Give a name for the font symbol.

2 Select the font.

3 Tick the style attributes you wish to apply.

4 Click to confirm.

▷ You can then use this symbol to create a shared asset (cf. 6.2 - E - Using shared assets).

6.2 Library

A-Using the Library

The Library stores all the symbols created and files imported into your movie. When you import a file, it is stored automatically in the Library as a symbol. The symbols can by classified into folders.

▷ **Window**
Library

Ctrl **L** (PC) or F11
⌘ **L** (Mac)

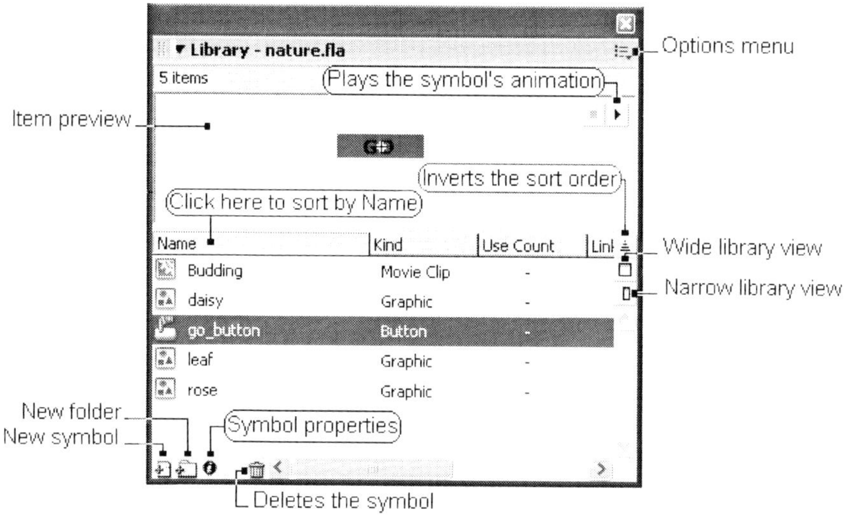

▷ To change the preview's background, choose one of the following options in its shortcut menu:

Movie's Background This uses the same background colour as the movie.

White Background This uses white as the background colour.

Show Grid This displays the grid.

▷ To put a Library item on the stage, drag it there: this creates a symbol instance.

OPTIMISATION

B - Managing Library items

▷ Select the symbol or folder and open the **Options** menu.

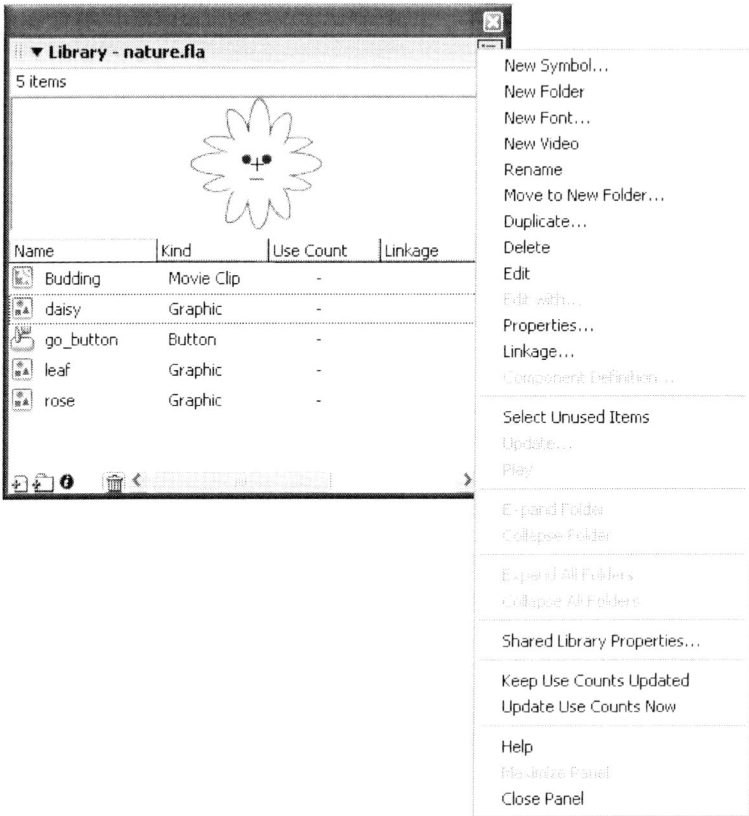

▷ You can rename an item, copy it, delete it, etc.

⇨ *Another way to delete a symbol is to click the button. If you delete a symbol, any instances of it placed on the stage will also be deleted.*

▷ To display an item's properties, click the icon.

▷ To look for Library items that are not used in your movie, use the **Select Unused Items** option.

▷ To find out how many instances are used, click the **Update Use Counts Now** option.

*The number of instances used appears in the **Use Count** column.*

▷ If you want these use counts to be updated automatically, activate the **Keep Use Counts Updated** option.

▷ To create a new folder, click the icon on the **Library** panel or choose the **New Folder** option in the **Options** menu.

▷ To insert items into a folder, select them and drag them into that folder.

▷ To move items quickly into a new folder, select the items you wish to move, display the shortcut menu and click **Move to New Folder**. Enter a **Name** for the folder and click **OK**.

The items move automatically into the newly-created folder.

▷ To open or close a folder, double-click it: to open or close all the folders, activate the **Expand All Folders** or **Collapse All Folders** option as is appropriate in the **Options** menu.

⇨ *The Library is linked to the active movie. To make symbols available for all your movies, you should use one of the common libraries or create links.*

C-Using a common library

Flash supplies several common libraries (buttons, sounds, etc...) but you can create others in order to use their symbols in other movies.

▷ **Window - Other Panels - Shared Libraries**

▷ Choose one of the libraries named in the list.

▷ Drag the symbol that interests you onto the stage or to the movie's Library.

⇨ *To create a common library, simply save the movie containing the library in the **Libraries** folder of Flash MX 2004: C:\Program Files\Macromedia\Flash MX 2004\First Run\Libraries (on a Mac, the First Run folder is inside the Macromedia Flash MX 2004 folder).*

⇨ *To delete a common library, simply remove the file containing it from the **Libraries** folder.*

D-Opening another movie's Library

▷ **File**
Import
Open External Library

Ctrl Shift **O** (PC)
⌘ Shift **O** (Mac)

▷ Double-click the movie containing the library you wish to open.

OPTIMISATION

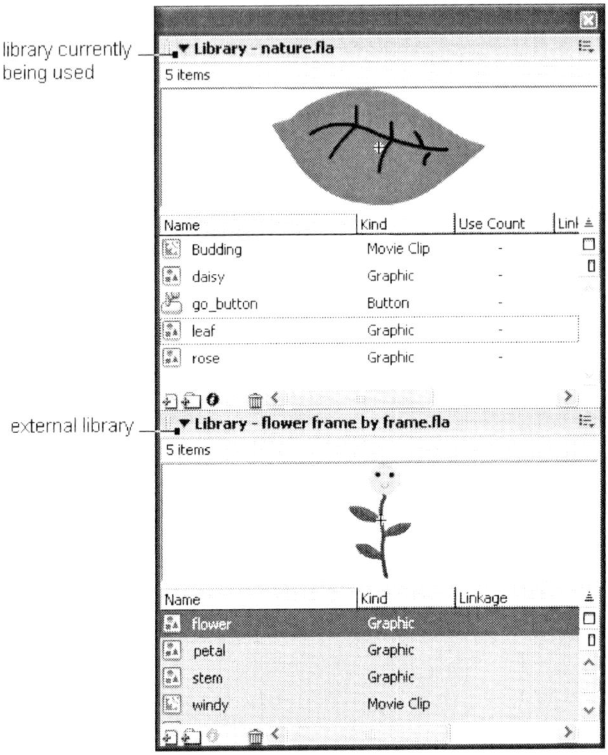

You can copy items from one library to another by dragging them.

⇨ *When you import or copy items that have the same name from one library to another, this dialog box appears, asking whether you want to replace the existing items or not:*

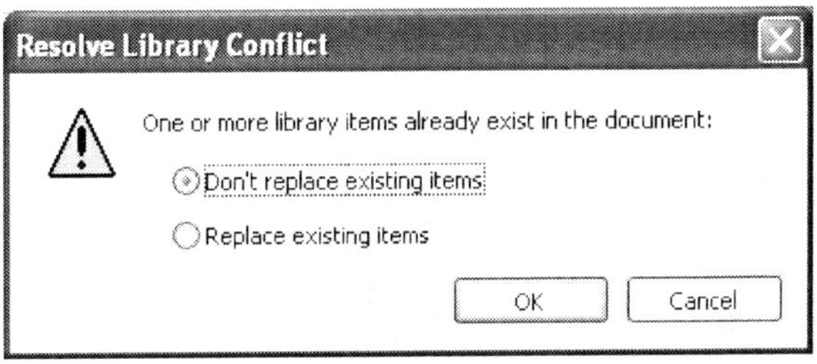

E - Using shared assets

Shared libraries contain ***shared assets****, which link symbols contained in the library of a published Flash movie (SWF format) to the symbols contained in the library of one or more other SWF Flash movies. With a* ***runtime shared asset****, the external items from the source file are loaded into the target file when that file plays. These links make it easier to update movies and to optimize resource management by sharing symbols contained in a single file.*

Creating a shared asset

▷ In the source movie, create the symbol that you want to link.

▷ Select the symbol you wish to link in the Library.

▷ Click the **Linkage** option in the **Options** menu.

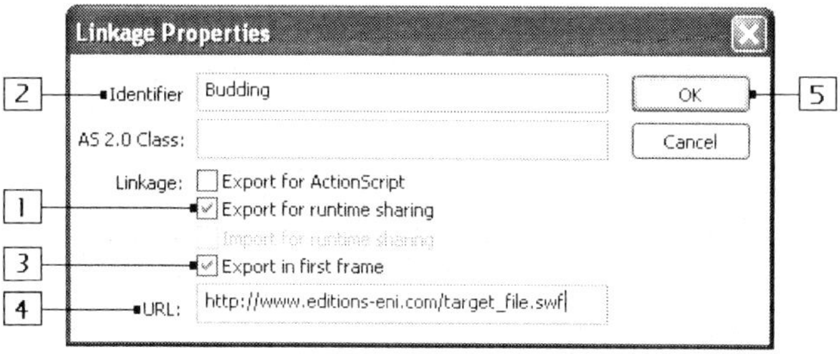

1 Tick this option.

2 Enter an identifier for the symbol (no spaces).

3 Deactivate this option if you do not want the symbol to load before the first frame of the movie.

4 Indicate the URL where the movie containing the shared asset (the target file) will be published.

5 Click to confirm.

▷ Save then publish your movie.

Linking a shared asset

▷ In the target movie's library, select the symbol that you want to link with the symbol from the source file.

▷ Click the **Options** menu then **Linkage**.

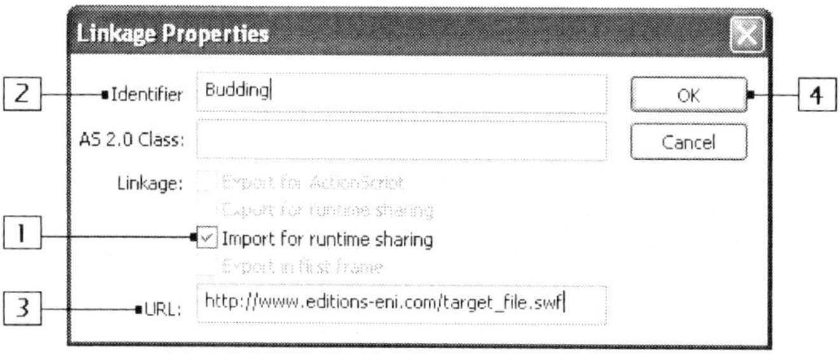

1 Tick this option.

2 Enter an identifier for the symbol, which must be identical to the identifier of the symbol in the source file.

3 Indicate the URL where the movie containing the asset you wish to share (the source file) is located.

4 Click to confirm.

▷ Save then publish your movie at the URL defined in the source movie.

*The links appear in the **Linkage** column in the Library.*

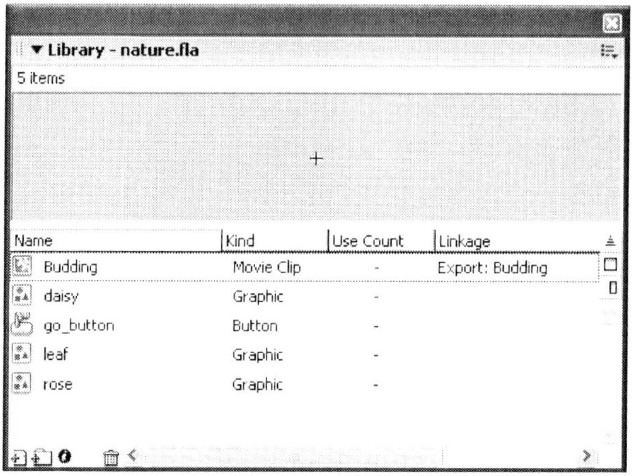

Breaking a link

▷ In the Library, select the symbol concerned.

▷ Click the **Options** menu then **Linkage**.

▷ In the **Linkage Properties** dialog box, deactivate the import or export option as appropriate.

▷ Click **OK**.

6.3 Movie structure

A - Managing scenes

A movie can be made up of several scenes, each of which is a "mini-movie".

▷ To display the scenes:

Window
Design Panels
Scene [Shift] [F2]

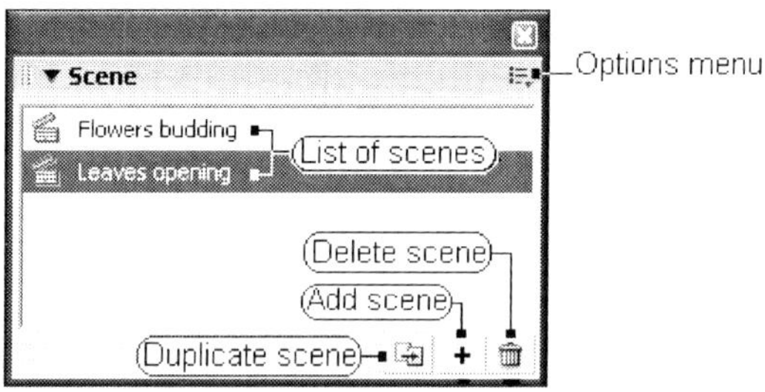

▷ To choose a scene, select it in the list on the **Scene** panel, or use the **View - Go to** menu or click the button on the **Edit** bar:

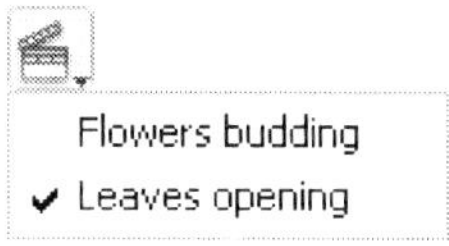

▷ To rename a scene, double-click its name in the **Scene** panel and type the new name.

▷ If you are not applying any scripts, the scenes will play in the order in which they appear in the **Scene** panel: to change this order, drag the scenes to the correct position in the list.

B - Using the Movie Explorer

*You can use the **Movie Explorer** to view the items that your movie contains in the form of a tree.*

▷ **Window**
Other Panels
Movie Explorer

[Alt][F3] (PC)
[⌥][F3] (Mac)

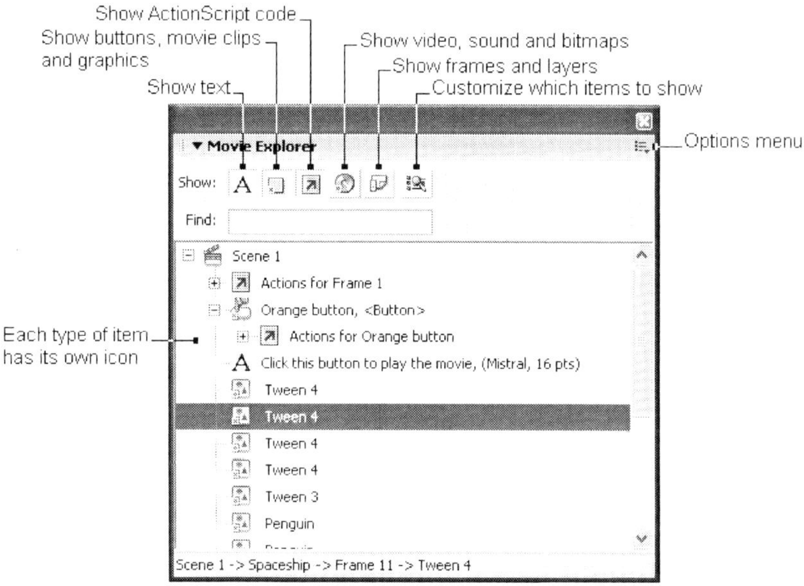

▷ To define what items are displayed in the Movie Explorer, open the **Options** menu and activate or deactivate these options: **Show Movie Elements**, **Show Symbol Definitions** and/or **Show All Scenes**.

▷ To expand or collapse a branch in the tree, click the + or − sign (PC), or click the triangle (Mac) or activate one of the options in the **Options** menu: **Expand Branch** or **Collapse Branch**. To expand only the active branch, select the **Collapse Others** option in the **Options** menu.

▷ To print the movie's tree, click the **Print** option in the **Options** menu.

Finding an item

▷ Enter the name of the item you are seeking (or its frame number) in the **Find** box.

▷ To access a layer, frame or scene rapidly, select the item in the Movie Explorer, open the **Options** menu and choose **Go to Location**.

▷ If the symbol definitions are displayed in the explorer, you can quickly access the parts of the symbol using the **Go to Symbol Definition** option in the **Options** menu.

C - Managing symbols in the Movie Explorer

▷ To modify a symbol in symbol-editing mode, double-click it.

▷ To see all the items that make up a symbol, activate the **Show Symbol Definitions** option in the **Options** menu.

▷ To select all the instances of a symbol in the Movie Explorer, select it in the **Symbol Definitions** section of the Explorer then activate the **Select Symbol Instances** option in the **Options** menu.

This selects the instances of the symbol that exist in the active scene.

⇨ *Use the **Options** menu to manage items in the Movie Explorer: **Rename, Edit in Place, Cut, Copy, Clear** etc. (if you remove an item it will be removed from the scene, but not deleted from the Library).*

7.1 Exportation

A-Exporting movies

By exporting a movie you can modify it in applications other than Flash. The following table shows you the available export formats:

File types	Extensions	PC	Mac
Adobe Illustrator Sequence	.ai	Yes	Yes
Animated GIF, GIF Sequence	.gif	Yes	Yes
WAV Audio (windows)	.wav	Yes	No
Bitmap Sequence	.bmp	Yes	No
DXF Sequence	.dxf	Yes	Yes
EMF Sequence (Extended metafile)	.emf	Yes	No
EPS 3.0 Sequence	.eps	Yes	Yes
Flash Movie (Flash Player)	.swf	Yes	Yes
JPEG Sequence	.jpg	Yes	Yes
PICT Sequence (Macintosh)	pct	No	Yes
PNG Sequence	.png	Yes	Yes
QuickTime	.mov	Yes	Yes
QuickTime Movie (Macintosh)	.mov	No	Yes
Windows AVI (Windows)	.avi	Yes	No
WMF Sequence (Windows Metafile)	.wmf	Yes	No

Exporting to "sequence" type files will create several distinct files.

▷ **File**
Export
Export Movie

Ctrl Alt ⇧Shift **S** (PC)
⌘ ⌥ ⇧Shift **S** (Mac)

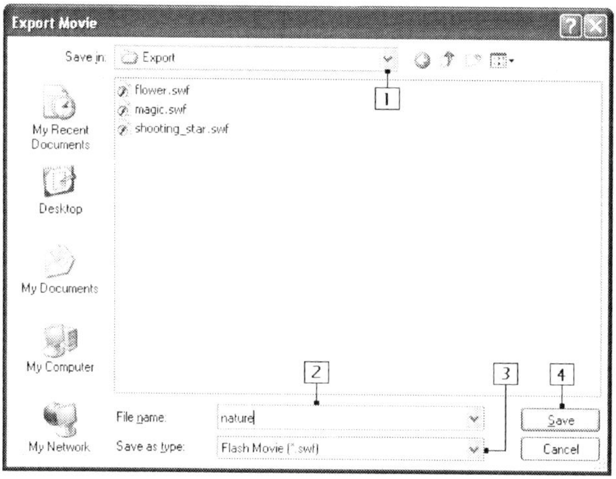

Under Windows

On a Mac

1 Select the folder in which you want to save.

2 Enter a name for the file.

3 Choose the required file format.

4 Start exporting.

The options in the dialog box below depend on the selected format.

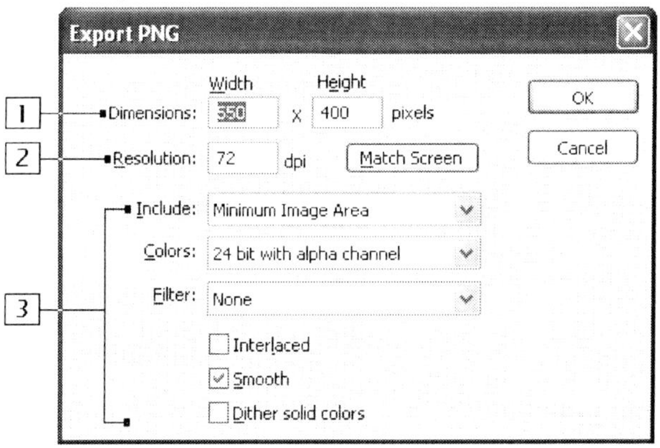

1 Enter the size of the exported movie (in pixels).

2 Set the resolution in dots per inch (dpi).

3 Next, choose the options related to the selected format (cf. below).

Settings for Bitmap format

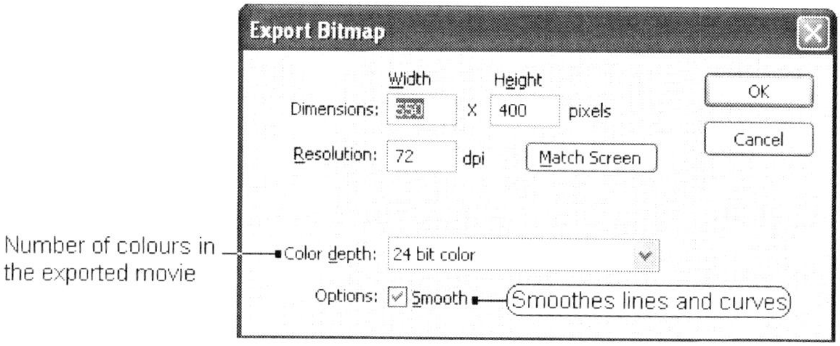

Settings for GIF format

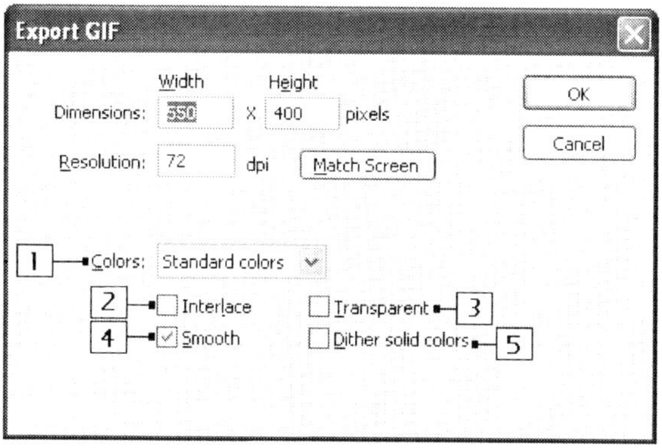

1 Select the number of colours for the exported movies (the **Standard colors** option corresponds to the 216-colour Websafe palette).

2 Tick this option if the image should appear progressively.

3 Tick this option to give the movie a transparent background.

4 Tick this option to smooth lines and shapes.

5 Tick this option to simulate colours in the movie that are not in the selected palette.

Settings for JPEG format

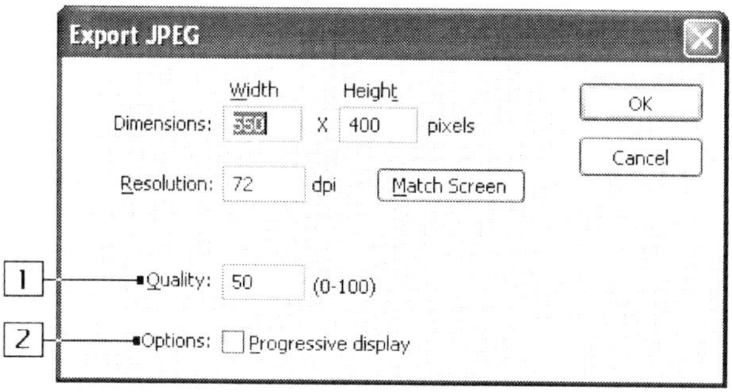

1 Enter a compression rate from 0 to 100 (the lower the **Quality**, the smaller the file size).

2 Tick this option if the image should appear progressively.

Settings for PNG format

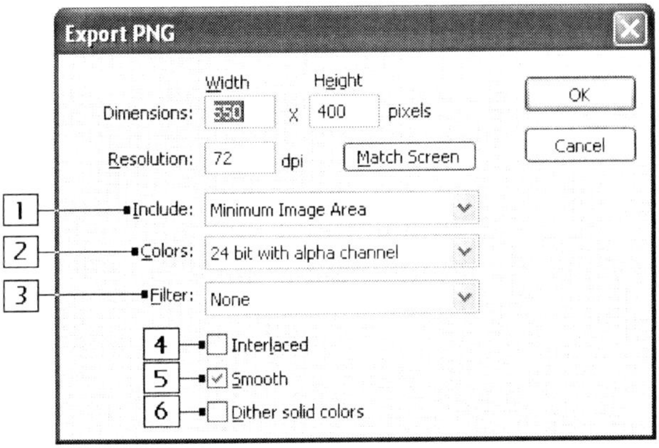

1 Specify which area of the stage should be exported: an area cordoned off by the items placed on the stage (**Minimum Image Area**) or the whole stage, no matter where the items on the stage are (**Full Document Size**).

2 Select the number of colours:

8 bit: 256 colours,
24 bit: thousands of colours,
24 bit with alpha channel: thousand of colours plus transparency.

3 If necessary, apply a filter to optimize file compression:

Sub/Up Compresses according to a calculation based on each pixel and the pixel directly before/above it.

Average Uses the average of two close-by pixels (left pixel and pixel above) to calculate a pixel's value.

Paeth calculates by three close-by pixels (left pixel, pixel above and upper left pixel) then retains the pixel closest to that value.

Adaptive creates a colour palette using the image colours.

4 Tick the **Interlaced** option if the image should appear progressively.

5 Tick the **Smooth** option to smooth lines and shapes.

6 Tick the **Dither solid colors** option to simulate colours in the movie that are not in the selected palette.

⇨ *Use the **File - Export Image** command to export only the frame where the playhead is positioned.*

B - Publishing a movie

You must first activate the publishing formats, then set the settings for each format and then start the publication.

▷ **File**
Publish Settings

Ctrl ⇧Shift F12 (PC)
⌥ ⇧Shift F12 (Mac)

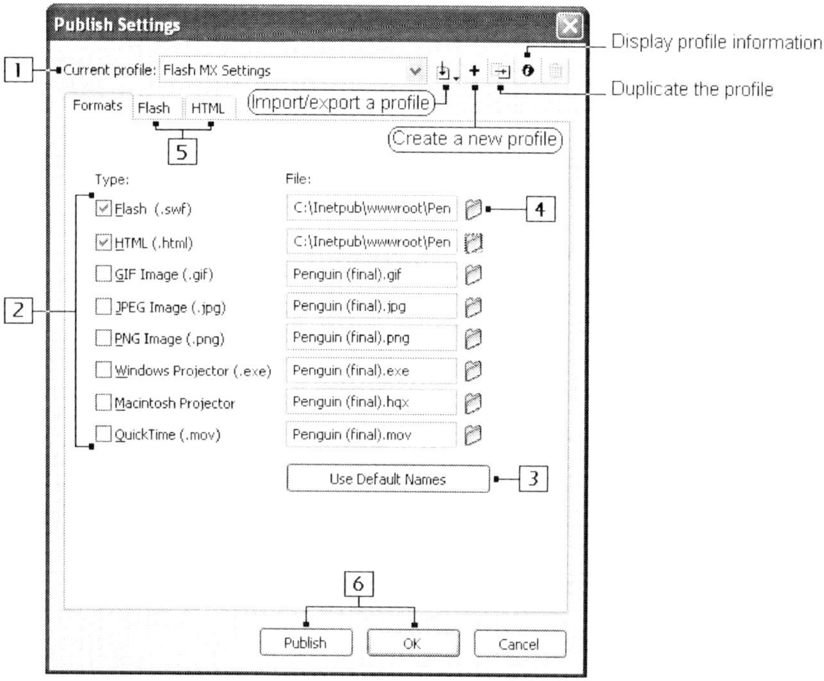

1 If necessary, select an existing profile.

2 Tick the required publishing formats: a tab appears for each format you tick. A Flash movie can be read by the Flash Player. The HTML format lets you integrate the movie into a web page. The **Windows Projector (.exe)** and **Macintosh Projector** formats create a movie that can be read without any particular player.

3 Click this button to apply the name of the movie file to the published file.

4 For each active format, click this icon if you want to choose a different saving folder from the one containing the source file.

5 Set the publish settings by clicking the tab concerned (cf. below).

6 Click **OK** to save the publish settings without publishing. Click **Publish** to publish the movie.

⇨ *The **File - Publish** command or* ⇧Shift F12 *publishes the movie with the active publication settings.*

PUBLICATION

Flash publication settings (.swf)

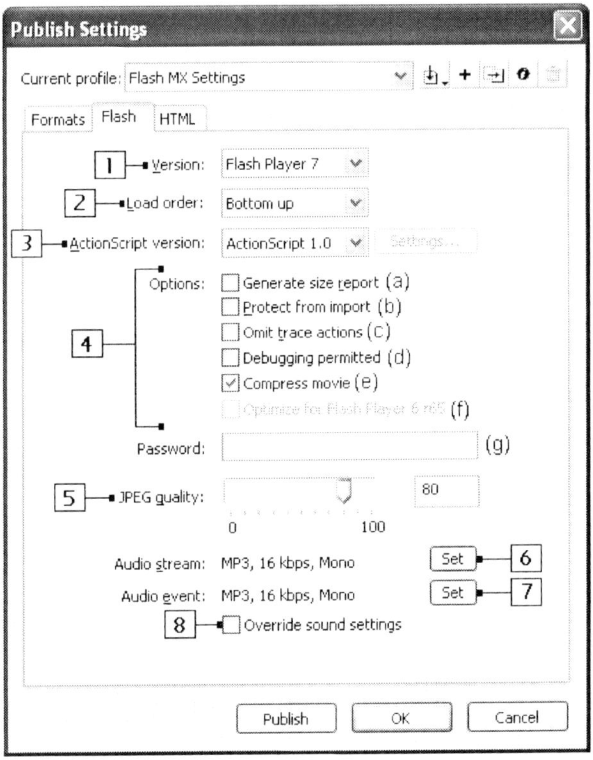

1 Choose which player version must be used to play the movie.

2 Set the layer load order.

3 If you are using ActionScript code in your movie, indicate the language version, **ActionScript 1.0** or **ActionScript 2.0**. The new version, **ActionScript 2.0**, uses a object-oriented programming approach, which makes code maintenance easier.

4 Set these options:

(a) To generate a text file containing the size of each frame, sequence or item.

(b) To prevent uses converting the movie back into Flash .fla format. This option also lets you protect the document with a password (g).

(c) To not display the **Trace** actions in the **Output** window when you test the movie.

(d) To be able to debug your Flash movie remotely, after it has been included in an HTML page. In field (g), enter a password to prevent other users from debugging your movie.

(e) To reduce the size of the published movie (it can only be played in Flash Player 6).

(f) If you want to be able to play the movie in version 6r65 players if you selected Flash Player 6.

5 Set the bitmap compression.

6 Set the **Bit rate**, **Compression** and **Quality** for streaming sounds in the movie.

7 Set the same settings for event sounds.

8 Activate this option if you want the audio settings defined in this dialog box to take priority over those defined in the Property inspector.

HTML publication settings (.html)

Publishing a movie in HTML format lets you include it in an HTML page. To integrate a SWF file into an HTML page, you must add certain HTML tags, such as Object (Internet Explorer) or Embed (Netscape Navigator); Flash creates these automatically.

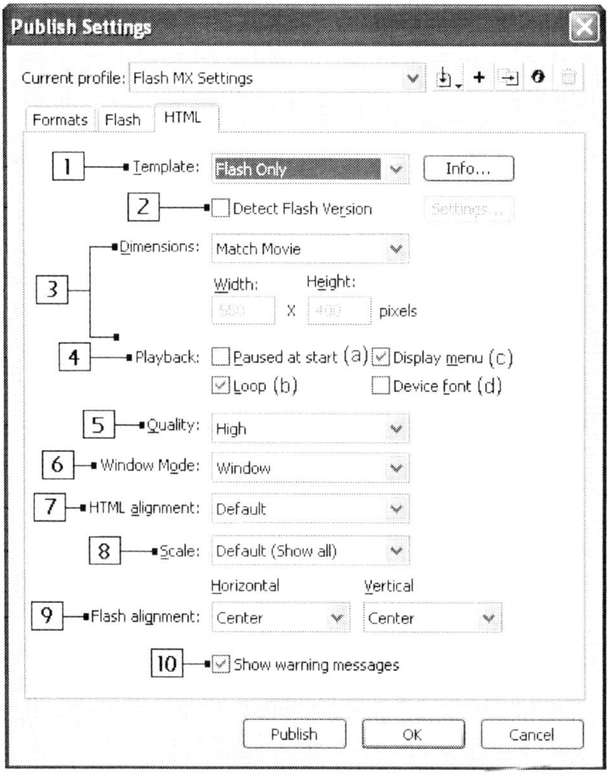

1 Select the HTML template in which Flash must embed your movie. The templates are saved in the Macromedia\Flash MX 2004\First Run\HTML folder (on a Mac, the First Run folder is inside the Macromedia Flash MX 2004 folder). If necessary, click the **Info** button to obtain information about the active template.

2 Tick this option to send the user to a player update web page if his or her current version is not compatible with the Flash document.

3 Select an option to set the WIDTH and HEIGHT values of the OBJECT and EMBED tags.

4 Set the play options:

(a) Tick this option to stop the movie playing automatically (the user will have to click a button or use an option to start the movie).

(b) To play the movie in a loop.

(c) The user will be able to display a shortcut menu to manage the movie.

(d) To allow the use of device fonts on static text blocks (Windows).

5 Set the anti-aliasing quality, finding a compromise between quality and processing speed:

Low	Flash Player applies no anti-aliasing.
Auto Low	Flash Player starts playing with no anti-aliasing, but activates it if it detects that the user's system can manage it.
Auto High	Flash Player starts playing with anti-aliasing, but turns it off if it detects that the user's system cannot manage it.
Medium	Anti-aliasing is applied but not on bitmaps.
High	Anti-aliasing is applied on non-animated bitmaps.
Best	Anti-aliasing is applied to the whole movie.

6 Set the display mode for the movie window in Microsoft Internet Explorer:

Window	The Flash movie can be played in its own window.
Opaque Windowless	The elements of the HTML page that are behind the movie will not be visible.
Transparent Windowless	The elements of the HTML page that are behind the movie will show through it.

7 Set the movie's position in the HTML document.

8 Use the **Scale** pop-up menu to position the movie within a specific area:

Default (Show all)	To display the whole movie in the specified area with its original proportions.
No border	To resize the movie to fit the specified area but keeping its original proportions.
Exact fit	To display the whole movie in the specified rea, changing the movie proportions if necessary.
No scale	To not resize the movie in the Flash Player window.

9 Set the horizontal and vertical alignment of the movie in the HTML page.

10 Tick this option if you want to see error messages in the case of any tag settings conflicts.

C - Previewing the movie before publishing it

▷ **File - Publish Preview**

*The active formats match those formats ticked under the **Formats** tab on the **Publish Settings** dialog box (cf. previous heading).*

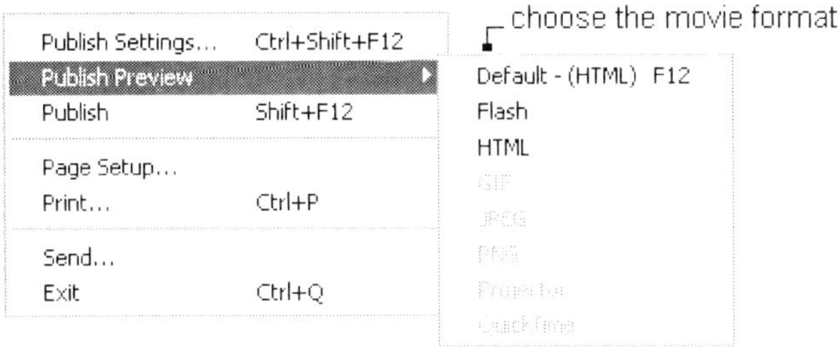

▷ The movie then plays in a window: close that window to leave the preview.

This command creates a file (whose format depends on the chosen option) and this is stored in the same folder as the Flash document.

D - Testing the movie

In Flash, you can test the movie to view it according to the defined publish settings, to find out its size, length, the bandwidth used, the frame sizes and so on.

▷ **Control** [Ctrl] [Enter] (PC)
Test Movie [⌘] [Enter] (Mac)

The movie plays on Flash Player in a window.

▷ To check the download performance, display the bandwidth profiler:

View [Ctrl] **B** (PC)
Bandwidth Profiler [⌘] **B** (Mac)

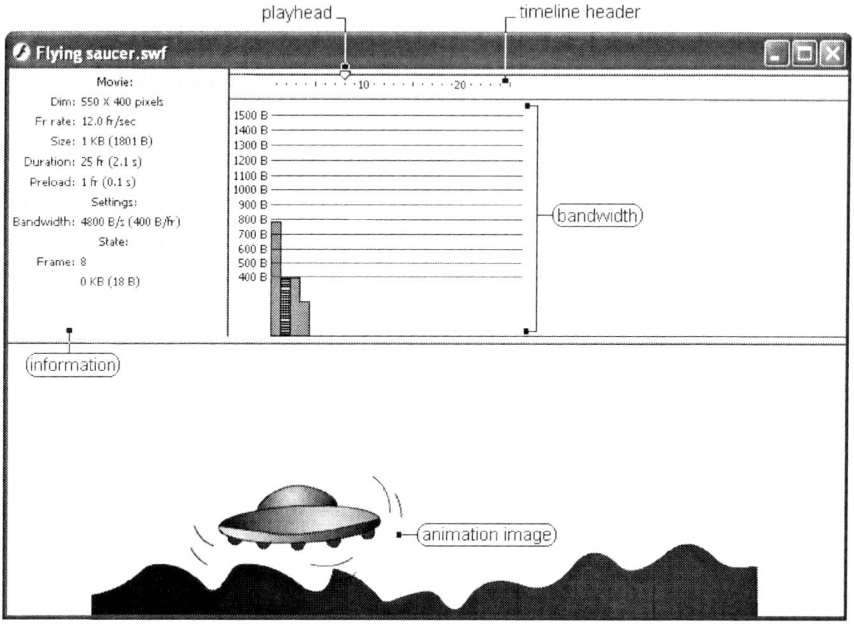

▷ To simulate a web server connection with streaming, using the speed indicated in the debugger:

View Ctrl Enter (PC)
Simulate Download ⌘ Enter (Mac)

▷ To change how data are displayed, use the options in the **View** menu:

Streaming Graph	To display the frames that make pauses while waiting for download.
Frame By Frame Graph	To display the size of each frame.

If a frame goes over the red line on the graph, Flash Player stops play until the frame has completely downloaded.

▷ Set the movie quality using **View - Quality**.

▷ You can choose a download speed in the **Debug** menu.

⇨ *To test a scene, use the **Control - Test Scene** command or* Ctrl Alt Enter *(PC) or* ⌘ ⌥ Enter *(Mac).*

A

B

C

D

E

INDEX

F

FILL

FINDING

FLASH MX 2004

FONT

FRAME

G

GIF

GRADIENT

GRID

GROUP

GUIDE

H

HTML

HYPERLINK

I

IMPORTING

INK BOTTLE

INSTANCE

J

JPEG

L

LAYER

LIBRARY

M

O

P

R

S

T

U

V

W

Z